MIA
HAMM
Soccer Player

FERGUSON
CAREER BIOGRAPHIES

MIA
HAMM

Soccer Player

Joan Axelrod-Contrada

Ferguson
An imprint of ☑ Facts On File

Mia Hamm: Soccer Player

Ferguson
An imprint of Facts On File, Inc.
132 West 31st Street
New York NY 10001

Library of Congress Cataloging-in-Publication Data
Axelrod-Contrada, Joan.
    Mia Hamm : soccer player / Joan Axelrod-Contrada.
        p. cm.
    Includes bibliographical references and index.
    ISBN 0-8160-5887-3 (hc : alk. paper)
    1. Hamm, Mia, 1972—Juvenile literature. 2. Soccer players—United States—
Biography—Juvenile literature. 3. Women soccer players—United States—
Biography—Juvenile literature. I. Title.
    GV942.7.H27A94 2005
    796.334′092—dc22   2004015046

Ferguson books are available at special discounts when purchased in bulk quantities for businesses, associations, institutions, or sales promotions. Please call our Special Sales Department in New York at (212) 967-8800 or (800) 322-8755.

You can find Ferguson on the World Wide Web at http://www.fergpubco.com

Text design by David Strelecky

Pages 107–123 adapted from Ferguson's *Encyclopedia of Careers and Vocational Guidance, Twelfth Edition*

Printed in the United States of America

MP Hermitage 10 9 8 7 6 5 4 3 2 1

This book is printed on acid-free paper.

CONTENTS

1

SUPERSTAR IN THE MAKING

Mia Hamm zoomed across the soccer field like a revved-up car.

She zigzagged past defenders, trapped the ball, and shot it forward a yard. Her opponent tried to recover the ball. But Mia, the speed demon, beat her to it. She had a mental quickness and hunger for victory that separated her from the pack.

Two coaches looked on in awe. John Cossaboon, who had picked Mia for his Olympic Youth Development Team, wanted to show off his latest find to Anson Dorrance, the coach of the U.S. Women's Soccer Team. Dorrance knew right away that 14-year-old Mia had a grasp of soccer well beyond her years.

"I saw this short-haired brunette just take off like she was shot out of a cannon," Dorrance recalled. "I just couldn't believe her athleticism."

Mia Hamm is one of the greatest soccer players of all time.
(Landov)

He predicted that someday Mia Hamm would become one of the greatest soccer players in the world. He was right. In the years that followed, Mia would become the top goal scorer, male or female, in the history of soccer. She would go on to lead the U.S. Women's Soccer Team to victory in the 1996 Olympics and 1999 World Cup. And, in the process, she would become a role model for millions of young soccer players. Mia would show them how to combine a killer instinct with a caring soul.

The Greatest Soccer Player in the World

Many people have asked Mia Hamm how it feels to be the greatest women's soccer player in the world. Mia hates the question. Humble and shy by nature, she has found it difficult to talk about her own accomplishments. She never thought she was the best. She was always striving to be better.

Mia has credited soccer with helping her grow as an athlete and as a person. Soccer, she said, taught her about teamwork, competition, and perseverance. It taught her how to budget her time, feel strong, and develop self-confidence. It taught her how to be mentally tough.

In life, as in soccer, Mia has had to overcome obstacles. Over the years, she has had to deal with scoring slumps, injuries, unwanted publicity, and the death of a beloved brother. At times, her desire to be the best has made her very critical of her own performance. Her confidence has suffered. But throughout it all, her love of soccer has kept her going.

As the first female team-sport superstar in America, Mia is a pioneer. She has faced different challenges than women in solo sports like golf or ice-skating. Mia does not just work to excel as an individual: She is always working to make the team stronger. She often deflects media attention away from herself onto her teammates. She says she owes everything to them.

Although widely hailed as the most popular female athlete in America, Mia never chose to be in the spotlight. People she trusted told her that soccer needed a "signature player" to popularize the sport. She has appeared in ads for Nike, Gatorade, and Mattel, winning new support for female athletes in corporate America. In the course of her career, she became the face of women's soccer.

Mia also used her fame to support causes close to her heart. She started her own foundation to fund research for bone-marrow disease and to champion women's sports. She reached out to girls who play soccer on Saturday mornings in recreation leagues across America.

Wherever Mia went, young girls clamored for her autograph. They greeted her by screaming her name as if she were a rock star. They showed up for her games with signs saying, "Girls Rule!" They wore her number 9 jersey and pulled their hair back in a ponytail like Mia. They went to sleep with her poster on their walls.

"It's very important for young girls to have female athletes they can identify with," Mia said. "It's another choice for them. They can say, 'I want to be a nurse. I want to be a doctor. I want to be a professional soccer player.'"

An Unusual Family

Mariel Margaret Hamm was born on March 17, 1972, in Selma, Alabama, to Bill Hamm, an Air Force pilot, and his wife Stephanie, a former ballerina. Stephanie called her daughter Mia after a favorite ballet teacher, Mia Slavenska.

Mia was born with a partial clubfoot requiring her to wear casts and orthotic shoes. But once the casts came off, Mia never slowed down. Mia grew up as the third of four daughters. First came older sisters, Tiffany and Lovdy, then Mia and younger sister Caroline. Two adopted brothers—one older, the other younger than Mia—followed.

The Hamms moved from place to place because of Bill's job. As a "military brat," Mia was always the new kid in the neighborhood. Throughout her childhood, the family moved from Alabama to California, Italy, Texas, and Virginia.

In the segregated world of Selma, Alabama, the Hamms stood apart. They belonged to a small black Catholic church because Bill Hamm wanted to experience life as black people knew it. During Lent, the Catholic season of fasting and prayer before Easter, the Hamms ate potato meal or unseasoned rice and lentils to prove they were no better than the poor people who had little else to eat.

Religion was an important part of life for the Hamms. Until she met Bill, Stephanie Hamm had originally wanted to be a nun. Although she decided to marry and raise a family, Stephanie was committed to her faith and dedicated herself to charitable causes. She taught ballet to girls in the garage of her church, and she also ran a home for unmarried mothers. Stephanie's commitment to the needs of others set a strong example for Mia, who would later use her celebrity in many positive ways.

A Sport for Warriors

Soccer got its start in ancient Greece as a sport to strengthen warriors for battle. Its popularity grew until soccer became known in modern times as "the world's game." The sport has long had a reputation for rigor and roughness.

Until the 1970s, few girls or women played the sport. Although soccer had been introduced to American college women in 1919, few women played it. Some people worried about the physical strain. They thought that if women played a rigorous sport, they might not be able to have children. Others thought women should stick to genteel sports like badminton rather than play ball in the dirt.

In the 1950s, many Americans moved to the suburbs, where grassy open fields beckoned boys, and sometimes their sisters, to play soccer. In 1964, the American Youth Soccer Association was born. In 1972 the year Mia was born, Congress passed Title IX, an amendment prohibiting sex discrimination at federally funded schools and colleges. The law gave women's sports equal footing with men's sports in terms of opportunity and funding. Soccer, as a competitive sport for women, was still in its infancy. But that was about to change.

The passage of Title IX gave women's sports a much-needed boost. Some colleges began to launch soccer programs. When coach Anson Dorrance first laid eyes on Mia Hamm, she was only 14 years old. But Mia had been playing soccer most of her life.

Early Childhood in Italy

In 1973, the Hamm family moved to Florence, Italy, where Bill was stationed for two years of overseas graduate study. Bill, an avid sports fan, tried to find an American sport like football or basketball on TV, but all he could find was soccer. Televised soccer games were the most popular shows in Italy. Thousands of fans went to local soccer games to cheer for their favorite teams.

At first Bill looked at this low-scoring game as just a tangle of bodies fighting for the ball. However, the more he watched, the more interested in soccer he became. He realized that everyone had a set position. Low scores were part of the game's charm. Each hard-earned goal was cause for celebration.

One day, Mia, who was about two, went to a park with her family, where she spotted an Italian man playing soccer with his son. She rushed in and kicked the ball. The man kicked it back to her. She booted it back, stealing the ball from the son. For nearly half an hour, Mia and the boy's father kicked the ball back and forth.

An Emotional Child

After two years in Italy, Bill was transferred back to the United States. The family spent a brief period in California, then moved to Wichita, Texas. Soccer, meanwhile, was gradually becoming more popular in the United States. The Hamms were delighted to learn that their new hometown of Wichita had a youth soccer league.

Bill became a coach and referee. He read every book he could find about soccer to familiarize himself with the rules and fundamentals of the game. Mia, however, was too young to play in the youth league alongside her older siblings. For a while, she needed to be content with chasing stray balls.

Although shy in public, Mia had a temper at home. Mia's family called it "The Curse." Mia would stomp off in a huff if she lost a game or if someone disagreed with her. Stephanie thought Mia needed a way to blow off steam. Ballet, she thought, would be perfect for the petite and well-coordinated Mia.

So, when Mia was about four years old, Stephanie brought her to a ballet class. Mia hated it. The pace of the class was too slow, and the slippers were too tight. She didn't want to go back.

Finally, at the age of five, Mia was old enough to join her older siblings in the PeeWee Soccer League. She now had a way to channel all her pent-up emotion. As part of a team, she felt an instant sense of belonging. She found that, once she started making goals, she didn't feel so shy anymore.

Brother Garrett

At about this time, Stephanie and Bill decided that, after four girls in a row, they wanted a son. They went to adopt one boy but came back with two: Garrett, an eight-year-old Thai-American orphan, and Martin, an infant of black and Puerto Rican descent. Mia instantly hit it off with her new big brother, Garrett.

Garrett shared her love of sports. He and Mia became constant companions. Whenever the neighborhood kids played ball, Garrett made sure Mia was on his team. Otherwise, no one would have wanted to pick the small, shy girl on the sidewalk. Garrett waved her in from the sidelines.

Garrett called her his "secret weapon." At first, the two would downplay the fact that Mia was fast and could catch the ball. Then, at a critical time in the game, they would give each other a look, and Mia would start playing hard. Together, they would win the game. Garrett's faith in Mia's athletic abilities gave her the confidence to play with the big kids.

2

PLAYING WITH THE BOYS

With her older brother, Garrett, at her side, Mia faced off against bigger, more powerful kids, most of whom were boys. Later, she would say that "playing up" was a key ingredient in her success.

The Hamm family spent much of Mia's childhood in Texas. Mia spent kindergarten through second grade in Wichita. She then moved to San Antonio for grades 3 to 5 before heading back to Wichita for grades 6 to 10. Playing sports helped Mia make friends. Her emotions now had an outlet. She could turn humiliation into a header, anger into a steal. Life, for her, seemed simplest inside the white lines of the soccer field.

"For this shy kid, sports was an easy way to make friends and express myself," Hamm wrote in her autobiography.

"While my mom and dad became very good at packing boxes, I found stability on the soccer field."

During recess, Mia practiced her skills on the hot Texas blacktop. She and her mostly male friends used whatever they could find for goals—shoes, cans, and basketball poles. Practicing on the hard pavement helped sharpen their skills. When the bell rang, Mia never wanted to go back inside.

"I'm sure that in my early years, my mom thought soccer meant skinned knees and 'often tardy' on my report cards," Mia said.

Growing up, Mia played a variety of sports on all-boys teams.

"It was either play with the boys or not play at all," she later wrote. "Most important, playing with boys helped me become competitive and develop that combative spirit I have today. . . . I truly believe that guys (much more so than girls) are taught to compete against one another and go after one another hard in practice and not apologize for success."

Knocked in the Stomach

When Mia was five or six years old, she learned one of her first lessons in soccer the hard way—by getting hit in the stomach with a soccer ball. The ball was coming at her fast, and, instead of trying to trap it, she let her stomach do the work. The ball stopped, practically knocking the wind out of her.

From that moment on, she started practicing the art of trapping. It's not an easy skill to learn, since the rules of soccer prohibit trapping the ball with what comes most

Mia has been a fierce competitor her whole life. (Getty Images)

naturally—your hands. Soccer players need to use other parts of their bodies, such as their thighs and the instep of their feet, to catch the ball. This is no easy task, but, like everything else, Mia learned it through practice.

Siblings Teach Persistence

From an early age, Mia loved to win. She hated losing with a passion. Sometimes she'd topple over board games. She'd flee soccer games with her siblings rather than face the humiliation of losing. She was always the one apologizing later. "I'm sorry," she'd say. "I'm so sorry."

Her older siblings, though, quickly got tired of this.

"Are you going to quit?" they'd ask.

They refused to let her play with them unless she was willing to stay no matter what. She would later credit them with teaching her persistence.

Professional Soccer

In 1981, when Mia was nine, her family went to visit her grandparents in the Washington, D.C., area and took in a professional soccer game. The Washington Diplomats of the North American Soccer League (a men's league that folded in 1984) were playing.

"I remember getting a free ball, the one with the stars on it," she later told *Sports Illustrated for Women.* "I always thought, 'Someday that's going to be me out there.'"

Perhaps Mia saw herself playing in a men's league since she was used to playing on boys' teams. At the time, no opportunities existed in women's soccer in the United States beyond the college level. Although more children were playing soccer, few Americans regarded soccer as a spectator sport worth watching on TV.

The Hamms, however, were the exception. They knew about the World Cup, which is like the Super Bowl of soccer. Every four years, nearly every nation in the world chooses a soccer team to qualify for World Cup competition. Over the course of a year, these teams play in regional tournaments to qualify for the final round of competition. In the final round, 16 teams play against each other until only two remain. Those two teams then compete for the World Cup.

The Hamms were disappointed that no American TV channels were broadcasting the 1982 World Cup. The United States team had failed to qualify for the final rounds of the tournament. But because the Hamms lived near the Mexican border, they were able to get a signal from a Mexican TV station. In Mexico, soccer was a big deal. Mia and her family watched the 1982 World Cup in Spanish. They marveled at the skill of the players.

During breaks, the Hamm children went outside to practice the moves they had seen on TV. (Mia would later advise young players to watch soccer on TV to improve their game.) In the final match, Italy beat West Germany 3-1. The Hamms' home away from home had won the World Cup.

Even though the World Cup was only for men, women's soccer was quickly gaining momentum. In 1982, the United States put together its first women's soccer team for international competition. The buzz was that soccer might one day become an Olympic event. Mia was growing up at a time of expanding opportunities. Still, at the age of 10, she had no idea that in five years she'd become the youngest member of the U.S. Women's Soccer Team.

Football Player

Mia played a variety of sports before committing herself exclusively to soccer. In addition to playing pointguard in basketball, she was one of the first girls in Wichita to play Little League baseball. In seventh grade, her male friends urged her to try out for the boys' football team. Her parents, as always, encouraged but did not push her to explore her interest.

Mia made the football team without any trouble, taking her place as cornerback and wide receiver. Some boys ridiculed her. They hated being beaten by a girl. But Mia held her own. The media showed up to interview her. Even at the age of 13, Mia disliked the spotlight. She answered questions from TV reporters to be polite but hated having attention focused on herself rather than the team. She decided not to go back to football in eighth grade.

Choosing Soccer

As Mia grew older, it became clear that soccer was her best sport. She played well on every team she joined but truly excelled in soccer. As her opponents got bigger and stronger, she got faster and smarter. She was fearless and hungry in her desire to win.

Her father shared Mia's competitive drive. He rewarded Mia with 50 cents for every goal she earned. Sometimes she scored four goals in one game, making her a standout in a low-scoring sport.

Many spectators never knew that the standout player was a girl. They'd spot the short-haired Mia outside the girls room. "Hey, the boys' restroom is over there," they'd say. She put up with the embarrassment to keep playing the game she loved.

Mia's early years of practice put her far ahead of most of her teammates. While they were still working on controlling the ball with their feet, she did so instinctively. This freed her up to focus on the mental part of the game. She was always thinking ahead. Once she got the ball, she knew exactly what she wanted to do with it.

Opponents quickly learned of her scoring prowess. To keep her away from the goal, they'd put two or three defenders on her. She'd outsmart them by realizing that, if two or three defenders were guarding her, two or three of her teammates must be open. Mia seemed to instinctively know where they were. She'd wait until the last possible moment before passing one of them the ball. From there, she'd rush in toward the goal. Sometimes she'd hit a header into the net.

In soccer, Mia could use her small size to her advantage to swerve around defenders. She stopped playing other sports to concentrate on soccer.

"I'm comfortable expressing myself through soccer," she said. "It has everything—fear, frustration, elation. It's the cornerstone of my identity."

By the time she was a teenager, Mia was ready for challenges above and beyond her local boys' soccer team. She started playing on club teams made up of the best players from several communities. She became one of the best soccer players in Texas.

All-Star Player

In 1985, when Mia was just 13, she was named a Texas all-star player in women's soccer. Now she could play in bigger tournaments and all-star tournaments across the state. She started meeting girls who shared her love of soccer.

"When I started competing with state teams, I found out I wasn't this freak," she said. "There were other girls out there that competed as hard as me and got upset at losing like me."

For young women like Mia, the timing couldn't have been better. Women's soccer and women's sports in general were becoming increasingly popular. Coaches started visiting regional tournaments in search of top players.

John Cossaboon was one of these coaches. Cossaboon coached the women's soccer Olympic development team, a squad of high school and college kids who served as a "pipeline" of talent for the U.S. team. He scoured regional tournaments in search of 16- and 17-year-olds he could recommend to the nation's top college programs.

At one of these tournaments in Dallas in 1986, Cossaboon spotted Mia Hamm. He couldn't take his eyes off her. She was the smallest player in the group but also the most skilled. She trapped a skyward ball and drilled it into the corner of the net. She winged perfect passes to her teammates. She flew toward the goal with obvious fire and determination. No one else on the field had her speed or feel for the game. Cossaboon wanted her for his team. Astounded that she was just 14, Cossaboon looked at Mia and saw the future of women's soccer.

"Skinny, gangly, faster than the wind—that was my first impression," Cossaboon said. "The athleticism just jumped out at you."

After the game, Cossaboon met with Mia and her parents. He told them that Mia was already as good as college players. Until she was old enough to go away to school, he wanted her to train with his Olympic Development squad.

This was a turning point for Mia. Before then, she had never thought about playing soccer much beyond high school. Soccer was just a game she played and enjoyed. Now a new world was opening up to her.

National Women's Team

Mia did so well as a member of the Olympic Development Team that Cossaboon knew she was ready for even bigger challenges. He contacted his friend, Anson Dorrance, the legendary coach of both the University of North Carolina women's team and the U.S. National Team. Cossaboon told him there was a player he just had to see.

Dorrance was naturally skeptical. Youth-league coaches contacted him all the time, telling him about the "next great player." But, since this recommendation came from Cossaboon, he decided to fly down to Louisiana to check out the new sensation. Dorrance told Cossaboon not to point out Mia. If she were as good as he said, he'd be able to spot her immediately.

In less than a minute, Dorrance spotted her.

"Is that Mia Hamm?" he asked.

Cossaboon nodded.

"Oh, my gosh," Dorrance said. He knew right then he wanted her to try out for his team. He invited her to an upcoming training camp that spring. He had never seen a player accelerate like she had. Dorrance still talks about how Mia took his breath away.

3

MAKING THE TEAM

Shortly after her 15th birthday, Mia arrived at U.S. Training Camp, feeling excited, nervous, and shy. She was the youngest and least experienced player at the camp. She couldn't help but feel a little intimidated.

Mia began her first day of training camp in the gym, working out with weights and other fitness equipment. This was totally new for her. Mia had always just played soccer.

"I thought I'd die," she later recalled.

Next, Mia followed the women to the soccer field for another two hours of drills and scrimmages. By the end of the day, Mia was exhausted. Her muscles ached.

Still, she loved being around such a competitive group of women. They fought for the ball like warriors. Mia was astounded by the players' grasp of the subtleties of the game. Seeing them up-close made her want to be better. She wanted to take her soccer skills to the next level.

Mia met another teenager, Kristine Lilly, who was also trying out for the team. The two became fast friends and talked about their plans for the future. Both wanted to go to the University of North Carolina and make the National Team. Mia came home with a new sense of purpose.

"She came back from camp and said she wanted to do two things," Mia's father later said. "Go to North Carolina [for college] and win the world championship."

Making the Team

Mia assumed she'd go to college first, then make the National Team. But the two happened in reverse order. That summer, she got a surprise call from Anson Dorrance. She had made the National Team. At 15, she became the youngest member of the squad.

Dorrance invited Mia to travel with the team to China. Because the National Women's Team was a shoestring operation, the players stayed in barracks-like housing. They lived on Snickers bars and Pop Tarts.

On August 3, 1987, Mia played her first game of international competition in the Chinese city of Tianjin. Thousands of Chinese fans packed the stands. Mia had never played in front of so many people. Dorrance brought her in as a substitute. She was so nervous, all she could think about was not screwing up. She didn't. The United States won the game 2-1.

Later that year, Mia got permission from school to take her winter break early so she could play with the National Team in Taiwan. Once again, she played alongside women whose skill level was more advanced than hers. These women trained on their own. After one of the games, Dorrance took Mia aside. He told her she could be the greatest soccer player in the world. But maybe she wasn't ready. She knew that, when she got home, she needed to start training on her own.

Strong Work Ethic

Mia returned home determined to do what she needed to do to stay on the team. She started training on her own. That summer, she left the house by 8:00 every morning to practice her shooting, dribbling, and passing.

"Her work ethic was above everyone else's," said Lou Pearce, who coached her for two years in Wichita Falls. "While the boys were sleeping till noon, she was out at 8:00 A.M. on the side of the high school, working for an hour and a half—30 minutes of foot drills warming up, 30 minutes of shooting, 30 minutes of running. The goal didn't have a net. She'd kick the ball where she wanted, and then she'd go get it, never walking, always jogging."

Sadly, Garrett could no longer be his sister's athletic partner. At the age of 16, he was diagnosed with aplastic anemia, a blood disease that caused his body to fail to produce enough platelets. Garrett had to stop playing sports. His condition was progressive. He could lead an almost normal life for now, but no one knew what the future would hold.

Moving to Virginia

Before Mia's junior year in high school, Bill Hamm got news once again that he was being transferred. This time the family would be moving to Burke, Virginia. Mia was sad to be leaving Wichita, where the family had lived longer than anywhere else. But Virginia was closer than Texas to North Carolina. Many of Mia's friends from the National Team went to the University of North Carolina.

Mia was itching to go off to college and convinced her parents and school authorities to let her double her course load so she could graduate early. Mia started her junior year at Lake Braddock High School in the fall of 1988. In Burke, soccer was a spring sport, so Mia played with a club team, the Braddock Road Shooting Stars, in the fall. Mia also continued to play for the National Team. She was so busy she had no time left over for dates or dances.

When spring came, Mia joined the Bruins, the Lake Braddock female soccer team. Since the girls had already formed a solid team, coach Carolyn Rice worried about how Mia would fit in. She feared that anyone good enough to play on the National Team might have an attitude. But

Mia (right) fights for the ball during a game at the 1989 U.S. Olympic Festival. (Getty Images)

Mia herself quickly laid such fears to rest. She lugged the team gear and gave herself the worst balls for practice. She downplayed her own accomplishments and accepted only brief praise.

Mia brought a special strength to the team. No one got past defenders better than Mia. When the Bruins qualified for the state tournament, her teammates knew they would be able to count on her. In the championship game, the opposing team tried to squeeze Mia into a corner, which was a big mistake. She stutter-stepped the ball to create a narrow gap between her two defenders. Mia rocketed a cross-pass to an open teammate who shot the ball into the net. Lake Braddock took the lead 2-0 and then went on to win the game 4-0. Mia and her teammates won the state championship.

A few weeks later, Mia graduated from high school. She rejoined the National Team for a match in Italy. Then it was time to get ready for college. In September of 1989, she headed off to the school she had always wanted to attend: the University of North Carolina (UNC) at Chapel Hill.

4

COLLEGE GROWTH

Mia was excited about going to the University of North Carolina but knew that she would miss her family. Her father was being transferred once again, this time back to Italy. With her parents overseas, coach Anson Dorrance became Mia's legal guardian.

"Next to Garrett, coach Anson Dorrance has probably been the most influential person in my life," Mia wrote in her autobiography. "In my early years on the National Team and then all through college, he was the driving force behind my growth as a player and a person."

Dorrance presided over a team with an unusual name: the Tar Heels. (During the Civil War, North Carolina was a leading producer of tar. It was also the home of soldiers who chose to fight rather than flee, almost as if their heels were firmly stuck to the tar of their home state. North Carolina became known as the Tar Heel State.)

Dorrance was a tough coach who disliked the notion that female athletes needed to value cooperation over competition. He created a system that fueled competition. After every drill, he ranked players and posted the results for everyone to see. He used the word "savage" as a compliment.

"Anson gave us the feeling it was okay to feel good about our success," Mia said. "You should want to win. . . . With Anson you didn't have to apologize for being good and wanting to be better."

Challenging Herself

Mia put extraordinary pressure on herself to excel. At times she became so nervous before big games that she would vomit. She was like a tightly wound coil that would spring into action on the soccer field.

Sometimes Mia's temper flared. She wanted everyone to perform perfectly. Other times she yelled at teammates who did not perform. The team captains would step in to smooth things over. Mia wanted the team to win.

But Mia was toughest of all on herself. If she didn't play well, her confidence suffered. One day Dorrance saw her struggling with the ball and said, "Mia, you're off balance." Mia took the criticism hard, thinking the worst.

"As players, when we are having a bad day, we tend to think in melodramatic terms, that we've lost it, that everything's gone wrong, but usually all you have to do is correct one small element of your game," Mia wrote. "Anson understood that and, as always, knew how to get me back on track."

Coach Dorrance was surprised by Mia's reaction to his criticism. He had simply meant that Mia needed to work on her balance. She was literally off balance. She needed to lower her center of gravity.

Dorrance helped Mia develop confidence by working on small, simple areas she could improve. But, throughout her career, maintaining self-confidence would be an issue for Mia.

Balancing Soccer with Schoolwork

Mia chose political science as her college major. She had grown up in a family that understood the role the political process played in people's everyday lives. Her parents believed that everyone was equal. They encouraged her to compete with boys and become a pioneer in women's sports.

Unlike some college athletes, Mia refused to coast academically. She consistently made the honor roll. But balancing schoolwork and soccer was no easy task. Sometimes, while traveling with the National Team, she had to do her schoolwork on the plane. At school, she forced herself to get up early to get her work done.

"I'm exhausted after a lot of training sessions," she told *Seventeen* magazine. "I'd rather wake up at 6:00 A.M. and study than fight to stay awake at night."

"Superfrosh"

Dorrance built the team at UNC into a winning dynasty. Year after year, the Tar Heels won the NCAA championship. Mia's old friend, Kristine Lilly, joined her as a fellow freshman in 1989. Returning players had helped keep the team undefeated since 1985. Mia didn't want to disappoint the team by making "freshman mistakes." She ran sprints in the park to train in the off-season.

Coach Dorrance spied her on one of her runs and left her a short, encouraging note. "The vision of a champion is someone who is bent over, drenched in sweat, at the point of exhaustion when nobody else is watching."

In Mia's freshman year, the UNC Tar Heels finished the regular season

Mia and UNC coach Anson Dorrance (Getty Images)

undefeated. The team faced off against its archrival, North Carolina State, for the Atlantic Coast Conference (ACC) championship. Even though the Tar Heels had won the national championship the year before, they had lost the ACC to the North Carolina State Wolfpack. UNC wanted to take back the championship.

UNC went into the tournament with the definite edge. But at first they failed to live up to their reputation. Their defense was surprisingly weak. North Carolina State slammed in three goals. Then Mia came to the rescue. She booted in two goals. Fellow freshman Kristine Lilly added two more. The Tar Heels beat North Carolina State 5-3. Mia was named Most Valuable Player of the tournament.

UNC went on to the NCAA tournament, where the Tar Heels once again faced off against the Wolfpack. Once again, the two "Superfrosh" Mia Hamm and Kristine Lilly knocked in winning goals. With Mia's help, UNC won its fourth straight NCAA tournament. When all the stats were added up at the end of the season, Mia, the youngest member of the team, won the top spot for scoring. She had made an amazing 21 goals.

But Mia wasn't satisfied. She wanted to be a more complete player—one who excelled on defense as well as offense. The players she most admired, such as hockey star Wayne Gretzky, played both well.

During the summer of 1990, Mia worked hard to improve her skills while traveling with the National Team. In a tournament against Norway, she scored her first goal of international competition. Then she drove in four more. Mia was making her mark on the National Team. The U.S. Team won all six games it played.

That summer, Mia learned that FIFA, the international soccer association, had approved a World Cup for women as well as men. This historic event was scheduled for November of 1991. Now Mia would have a chance to play in the kind of competition she had watched on TV with her family growing up in Texas. She headed back to UNC in the fall of 1990, feeling excited about the Tar Heels' upcoming season and first ever Women's World Cup.

Sophomore Year

In the fall of 1990, Mia returned to Chapel Hill as a sophomore, ready for another season with the Tar Heels. No longer was she a newcomer. Because some of the top players had graduated, the team was left with a deficit of experience. Before long, the inexperience showed.

On September 22, 1990, the Tar Heels traveled to Connecticut for a game against the University of Connecticut (UConn) Huskies. The Huskies played aggressively, and some began to think that maybe UNC wasn't unbeatable after all. Mia kept her focus and kicked in two goals.

Nevertheless, the team lost in overtime, 3-2. The defeat was a crushing blow. The Tar Heels' remarkable 103-game winning streak had come to a close.

The effects of the loss lingered into the next game. The Tar Heels lacked their usual fire. In their game against George Mason, the Tar Heels missed several attempts to score a goal. The Tar Heels felt frustrated by all the saves by the George Mason goalkeeper.

Time was running out. With only 15 seconds left in the game, Mia refused to give up. She fought back her own doubts to lead the team to victory. She forced a George Mason player to make a bad pass so she could intercept it. The strategy worked. Mia gathered up the loose ball and raced toward the goal. Then she faked a shot. The goalkeeper dove one way, and the ball rolled in the other. Mia had save the day.

Mia's winning goal reenergized the team and established her as a leader.

Like a Light Switch

Every semester, Anson Dorrance scheduled conferences with his players to talk about their goals. Those meetings always made Mia nervous. She wanted her goals to be ambitious enough to be challenging but realistic enough to be attainable.

Mia went into her sophomore year conference without a clear idea of what she wanted to say. She didn't know what she wanted to do next. She sat across from Dorrance at his cluttered desk, feeling uncertain. She tried to avoid the topic. But Dorrance brought her back to the question of goals. What did she want?

"To be the best," Mia blurted out. She couldn't believe she had said that. "This semester one of my goals is to be the best."

He asked her if she knew what that meant. Mia started to sweat. She avoided eye contact. She fiddled with the upholstery on her chair.

Then Dorrance got up and walked over to the light switch on the wall behind her. He turned off the light. For a second, they sat in darkness. Then he turned the light back on. "It's just a decision," he said. "But you have to make it every day."

Dorrance meant that every morning when Mia woke up, she needed to choose between mediocrity and excellence. She had to reach for the best. She had to work hard to live up to her dreams.

Years later, Mia contributed an essay about this life-altering event to a book (edited by Marlo Thomas) called *The Right Words at the Right Time*: "Being the best is a simple decision, like flipping a light switch," she wrote. "It's not glamorous. It's not about glory or God-given talent. It's about commitment, plain and simple."

NCAA Championship

With Mia now a leader on the team, the Tar Heels made it easily into the NCAA finals. UNC would be squaring off against their former rivals, the UConn Huskies. The Tar Heels wanted to avenge their old loss. They wanted to prove, once and for all, that they were the best team.

"Coach told us to remember who we are and what it means to play for North Carolina," Mia recalled. "We wanted to bury them psychologically in the first fifteen minutes, and that's exactly what we did."

The Tar Heels played with intense focus and athleticism. They beat UConn 6-0. North Carolina had won its fifth straight NCAA title.

When the statistics were tallied up for the year, Mia led the entire NCAA in scoring with 24 goals and 19 assists. But, true to form, she played down her own accomplishments. The team always came first. "I always make sure I thank or hug the person who gave me an assist on a goal because the point belongs to her as much as me," she said.

The end of the fall season was bittersweet for Mia. She decided to take time off from school to participate in the upcoming World Cup tournament. Leaving college was a difficult decision. If she remained at UNC, she would

Mia (second from right) and some of her UNC teammates. Taking a leave from UNC, and her friends, to prepare for the World Cup was a tough decision for Mia. (Getty Images)

undoubtedly be the focal point of the Tar Heels' offense. But competing in the World Cup would give her a chance to work on her defense. Ultimately, Mia wanted to become the most complete player she could be. Thus, she chose to take a leave of absence from UNC and focus on the World Cup.

5

PIONEER

For Mia, the 1991 Women's World Cup tournament was a dream come true. "A World Cup for women was what we'd all dreamed about, and now we were on our way," she says.

Now female soccer players would have the same kind of championship as their male counterparts. Women's soccer had achieved a new level of seriousness. The U.S. National Team had a chance to make history. Mia and her teammates were pioneers.

Building Team Spirit

In early January 1991, Mia and her teammates, along with coach Dorrance, began training for the World Cup competition. The players received room and board but no salary. They spent the next several months training and playing in regional tournaments.

Getting together in the winter, rather than the spring, helped the Americans build cohesiveness. Mia was the youngest member of the team and looked up to veteran players like April Heinrichs, Michelle Akers, and Carin Gabarra. The team bonded off the field as well as on it. For example, while training in Haiti, the electricity went out in their hotel. The women kept each other company, staying up late and playing cards by candlelight.

Dorrance required that all the women training for the World Cup try out for their positions. At first, Mia was named reserve forward. She had played forward since high school and so was familiar with the position. Then one of the starting defenders got injured. Mia was assigned to a new position—right midfielder—with strong defensive responsibilities. Now she would definitely have to improve her defensive skills. She would also be able to use her old skills in new ways. If the player she was marking lost control of the ball, Mia could instantly turn on the offensive side of her game.

Going into the 1991 World Cup, the American women were a young, fit, and scrappy group. Observers praised their hard-driving "cowboy" spirit.

Still, hardly anyone expected the U.S. team to win. Soccer in the U.S. lagged behind that of other countries. The men's soccer team had failed to even place in the World Cup in the past 40 years. Women's soccer was just getting started as a serious sport.

April Heinrichs gives Mia a hug before a game. Heinrichs played for, and later became coach of, the Women's National Team. (Landov)

An Event Like No Other

The U.S. National Team did well at first but then faltered in a series of exhibition games leading up to the big match in November. Coach Dorrance knew the team would have to play better to win the World Cup. He abandoned his conservative defense-oriented approach and gave Mia and fellow midfielder Kristine Lilly permission to go on the attack. Mia knew that she could count on Lilly, who had also left UNC at the last minute to join up with the U.S. team.

The team arrived in China in mid-November. Mia and her teammates knew as soon as they arrived that this was an event like no other. They stayed in a luxury hotel and played in front of huge crowds. Some 65,000 people attended the event. Mia and her teammates had never played in front of so many people. Friends and relatives saw for the first time that women's soccer was a big deal. The World Cup was a whole new ballgame.

Ever Humble

Mia did well in her new position. On November 19, 1991, the U.S. National Team played their first World Cup game against Sweden. As usual, Mia downplayed her own accomplishments. She was quicker to point out her mistakes.

"The girl I was marking took me to school," Mia said about her Swedish opponent. But Mia failed to mention that she had scored the winning goal. The U.S. team beat Sweden 3-2.

On November 27 the U.S. team took on Germany. Mia and Kristine Lilly kept the ball on the other end of the field almost the entire game, showing off impressive defensive skills. Mia was becoming a more complete player. The U.S. team beat Germany 5-2 and was now on its way to the finals.

On November 30 the U.S. National Team faced off against heavily favored Norway for the World Cup. The Norwegians had the edge going in since they had beaten the American women in earlier games. But the Chinese crowd cheered for the Americans. They were the underdogs, the "Cinderella" team.

Mia and her teammates felt bolstered by the crowd but knew this would be the toughest game yet. Mia raced all over the field, disrupting Norway's offense. She saw Norway's offensive plays developing and broke them up before they got started.

But time was running out. The score was tied 1-1. Norway hoped to defeat the exhausted Americans in overtime. Then Michelle Akers, one of Mia's role models, summoned up her reserves of energy to make a spectacular play. Mia admired Akers for her composure and focus. With three minutes left to play, Akers calmly booted the ball into the net and scored a goal.

But the game wasn't over. The Norwegians tried to get the ball downfield, but Mia and her teammates drove them away. Then the whistle blew. The United States won the game 2-1. The American women were now world champions.

Mia and her teammates rushed onto the field, laughing and crying and hugging each other. Coach Dorrance joined them in celebration. The American women had won the first-ever World Cup. No American team, male or female, had ever won a world championship in soccer. The U.S. Women's National Team had made history.

No Fanfare at Home

Back home, though, few people seemed to care. Only one reporter met the team at the airport. Many publications did not mention the World Cup at all. *Sports Illustrated* gave the event only a brief mention in its scorecard section. One sponsor took out an ad to tell the story that so many newspapers had missed. The World Cup barely existed, as far as the American media was concerned.

But the players themselves knew what they had accomplished. They had proven they were the best women soccer players in the world. They had played their hearts out without any incentives of fame or fortune. They had shown that hard work and dedication pay off.

"For the first time the world knew there was something unique happening in American women's soccer," Mia wrote. "By winning that tournament, we kicked open the door for women's soccer and let in millions of girls who could now brag that American women were the best soccer players in the world."

Back to College

Mia headed back to Chapel Hill, eager to get back to school for the spring semester. Her teammates and coach were her second family. She also began dating a young man named Christiaan Corry, whom she met in a political science class. Christiaan reminded her of her father with his intensity and easy wit. Also, like her father, he had chosen a military career. He was on his way to Marine flight school.

Mia and several of her roommates shared an off-campus apartment. Living together made them even closer.

The roommates played Nintendo and watched sports on TV. The apartment was dubbed "Animal House" for its constant state of disarray. Between soccer and schoolwork, sometimes Mia didn't have time to unpack her suitcase.

The Tar Heels looked especially promising in the fall of 1992. Dorrance had made the team into a winning machine. "We had a combination of players that clicked so well off the field that our bonding translated on the field into a devastating, unselfish attack," Mia said. "We all pushed one another to be better."

Mia came back from the World Cup a vastly improved and more versatile player. The official World Cup report had cited her for being one of the best attacking defenders in the tournament. Mia had a better understanding of how to help her teammates when she couldn't score. She also took it on herself to rally the troops. In one memorable game against Duke, the Tar Heels lost their lead at the top of the second half.

"The last emotion you want to display to your teammates is one of disappointment," Mia later said. "It was my job to motivate the other players. There was still a lot of time left." UNC won the game 3-1, thanks largely to three spectacular assists by Mia. One month later, UNC met up with Duke again. This time the NCAA championship was at stake.

Again, Duke got into a leading position, but Mia refused to panic. Instead, she drove the ball into the goal to tie up the score. Then UNC got on a roll. One more goal, then another by Mia. The team just kept on scoring. Coach Dorrance took Mia out of the game to give her a rest, but she begged him to put her back in. It was Kristine Lilly's last game, and Mia wanted to be on the field with her. Dorrance relented. With 18 minutes remaining, Mia scored her third goal of the match. UNC won by a spectacular 9-1. In the low-scoring game of soccer, this was an amazing accomplishment.

Years later, Mia looked back at this game as a particularly memorable one. "It was Kristine Lilly's last college game, and even though I won another championship the next year as a senior, that NCAA title my junior year remains among my greatest triumphs on the soccer field," she wrote.

"Top Gun" of Women's College Soccer

People magazine dubbed Mia the "top gun of women's college soccer" in 1993. After her spectacular 1992 season, Mia won the Most Valuable Player Award from both the ACC and NCAA. She led the nation in scoring with a record 92 points and 33 assists.

Mia's senior year was just as phenomenal. Again, UNC won the NCAA title, and Mia won the same awards as the previous year. In addition, she won the Honda Broderick Cup as the outstanding female athlete in all of college sports.

But the statistics and awards told only part of the story. Mia played with the grace of a ballerina and the courage of a bullfighter. Her accelerations put people on the edge of their seats. She cut through the tightest of spaces. Mia was more than just a scoring machine. She was also a marvel to watch.

Final College Game

In the final game of Mia's college career, UNC faced off against George Mason University for the NCAA championship. Some 6,000 fans packed the stands to watch Mia play her last college game. It was the largest crowd ever to watch a women's soccer match in the United States.

The Tar Heels went in determined to win their eighth straight NCAA championship. George Mason didn't have a chance. In the first half, UNC scored twice, with Mia assisting on one of the goals. Then, in the second half, she stole the ball from George Mason and redirected it to the other end of the field. She whizzed past defenders and drilled the ball into the net. Mia had just made the last goal of her college career. The crowd went wild.

Late in the game, coach Dorrance pulled Mia out so she could rest. As she jogged back to the bench, the crowd gave her a standing ovation. Mia was overwhelmed with emotion, but, as usual, she used the opportunity to praise her teammates rather than bask in her own glory. She attributed her success to the strength of the program at UNC.

"The goals and the championships are nice, but the emotions, the tears, and the smiles on my teammates' faces are my championships," she said.

Olympic Women's Soccer

One of the most memorable experiences of Mia's senior year took place off the soccer field. She and her roommates were sitting around watching sports on TV when the phone rang. One of the women answered, listened for a minute, and started screaming. Women's soccer had just been added to the lineup for the 1996 Olympics.

First the World Cup, now the Olympics: Mia couldn't believe her luck. Women's soccer was finally getting its fair due. "You hear all the clichés that it's a dream come true," she said. "Well, it is for myself and for every young girl growing up who plays a sport."

"Field of Dreams"

In February of 1994, Mia's UNC number 9 jersey was retired. She and Kristine Lilly, whose number was also being retired, were invited to a halftime ceremony along with fellow UNC alum Michael Jordan.

"For a school or team to retire your number is the ulti-mate compliment, and being there with Kristine made it even more emotional," Mia said. "Everything that I felt

When Mia left UNC, the school retired her number 9 jersey.
(Getty Images)

about UNC and its community came out that night, and Kristine and I were both choking back the tears."

As her graduation approached in May, Mia felt sad to be leaving the University of North Carolina. She called UNC her "field of dreams." Still, she was ready to move on.

"I don't want to sit and look at all the trophies," she said. "I don't want to live in the past—I want to live now."

6

RISING STAR

Mia had a job waiting for her once she graduated from college. In 1994, the U.S. Soccer Federation approved small salaries and a six-month residential camp for members of the U.S. Women's Team. The women had proven themselves as winners and began to be treated as such. Earning a salary for the first time was a huge relief for veteran players who had risked losing their jobs to play soccer. As pioneers, these women paved the way for other women to make soccer their career.

For members of the National Team, a career in soccer meant extensive travel. Some of Mia's teammates were married. On December 17, 1994, she joined them in the challenge of juggling a soccer career with marriage when she married her college sweetheart, Christiaan Corry.

Rise of Soccer

By the mid-1990s, soccer had become the fastest growing sport in the United States. Millions of girls and young women now played soccer. In 1994, the Men's World Cup was held in the United States, shining the spotlight on the National Team. Mia was one of the few women players featured in a new line of soccer trading cards. Corporations started looking for female soccer players to endorse their products. In 1994 Mia signed a contract with Nike.

Magazines found that young players loved reading stories about soccer stars like Mia Hamm and Michelle Akers. In the early 1990s, Akers was widely regarded as the greatest female soccer player in the world. Then, in 1993, Akers was diagnosed with chronic fatigue syndrome. She continued to play on the National Team but needed to conserve her energy.

Fellow veteran player April Heinrichs, meanwhile, had traded in her playing for a coaching career. In 1994, she became assistant coach of the Women's National Team.

New Coach

Undoubtedly the biggest change for Mia during this time was the departure of Anson Dorrance as coach of the National Team. Dorrance had decided that he couldn't continue to coach both the U.S. team and the University of North Carolina team. In August 1994, he surprised many by announcing that he was stepping down as coach of the National Team to concentrate his efforts on UNC.

Dorrance turned over his coaching responsibilities to Tony DiCicco, the team's popular goalkeeper coach.

DiCicco believed wholeheartedly in women's sports. He had grown up with a strong mother who shot baskets with him in the driveway. She showed him by example that women could be active participants, rather than just spectators, in sports. After college, DiCicco played professional soccer for five years with the American Soccer League. Then, in 1991, he joined the women's National Team as goalkeeper coach. As the new head coach, he planned to continue the winning formula Dorrance had set in place.

But because Mia was so attached to Dorrance, any new coach would be an adjustment for her. Author and *New York Times* sportswriter Jere Longman observed that Mia and DiCicco were a lot alike. Both were reserved on the surface but deeply emotional underneath.

On April 11, 1995, during a match between the United States and Italy, Mia and DiCicco got into an argument on the field. Mia accused DiCicco of over-coaching fellow player Tiffany Roberts in midfield. DiCicco felt that Mia was being disrespectful. "Worry about your own game," he said. "It needs work."

The next day, DiCicco told Mia she was right: He *had* been over-coaching Roberts. Mia, in turn, apologized for yelling at him. The talk helped their relationship develop into one of mutual admiration.

Mia gave DiCicco the words he used to guide him as a coach: "Coach us like men but treat us like women." DiCicco tried to coach positively, so players would feel inspired to play their best.

Before the 1995 World Cup, coach DiCicco sensed a certain tentativeness in some of the players. He wanted to bring in a sports psychologist to give his team the mental edge. But officials at the U.S. Soccer Federation laughed at his request. They did not take sports psychology seriously.

Mia, however, knew that her emotions could work either for her or against her. She had a burning desire to win. Her passion drove her to succeed. But her standards were so high, she could not always meet them. And, when she didn't, her confidence suffered. She played less aggressively. She had to build herself back up.

Still, Mia's good days more than compensated for her bad ones. In 1995, she scored the most goals and assists of anyone on the team. People started saying she was the best female player in soccer. Mia, of course, disagreed, saying that she was far from being the best player on her team, let alone in the whole sport. But many observers disagreed.

The 1995 World Cup

The 1995 World Cup in Sweden generated far more attention in the United States than the 1991 World Cup had. For the first time, the matches would be broadcast on ESPN.

Going into the World Cup, the U.S. women looked strong. But their opening game against China ended in a tie. The U.S. team needed to win its next game to move ahead in the competition. The U.S. team was leading 2-0 when Mia faced one of the scariest moments of her career.

With only six minutes remaining in the game, assistant coach April Heinrichs took Mia aside and asked her to do something she had never done before: Play goalkeeper. The team's regular goalkeeper Briana Scurry had been evicted from the game for a technical violation. The United States had already used up all its substitutions. Mia knew she had to do what was best for the team, so she took over as goalkeeper.

Moments later, Denmark was awarded a free kick. Mia felt like she was up against a player who would have liked to blast her halfway across the Atlantic.

Fortunately for Mia, the ball flew over the net. The next time, though, she wasn't so lucky. During the final seconds of the game, a Danish player fired a hard shot her way. Mia blocked the ball with her stomach. It was a tough, courageous save. The U.S. won 2-0.

Mia later admitted to being scared to death. "The goal is much bigger when you're inside it than when you're shooting at it," she observed. Even though playing goalkeeper had been a scary assignment for Mia, she had once again proven her versatility as a player.

Mental Toughness

Mia agreed with DiCicco about the importance of the mental aspects of the game. When kids asked her about the most important skill for a soccer player, she always gave the same answer: "Mental toughness."

A few days after their victory over Denmark, the U.S. women squared off against Australia in a game that exemplified mental toughness. The number of goals scored would determine who would move into the next round of competition. The U.S. needed to score more goals than China, which was playing its own game against Denmark.

The U.S. kept tabs on the China game by cell phone. The U.S. was leading Australia 2-1 when the cell phone rang. China had just scored another goal.

"One more! We need one more!" DiCicco yelled.

The U.S. team went into attack mode. Finally, two minutes into stoppage time, Mia dribbled in the penalty box and was fouled. Carla Overbeck then drove the ball into the net on a penalty kick, bringing the score up to 3-1.

Then the cell phone rang again. China had scored again. The U.S. women needed to dig into their energy reserves and score yet another goal. Debbie Keller scored the team's fourth goal. The U.S. women had scored an incredible four goals in the second half against Australia.

"We did this because every player truly believed we could and took action to make it happen," Mia wrote. "That was mental toughness."

But, in a subsequent game against Norway, the U.S. team lacked the mental toughness needed to win. Instead of making their own chances, the U.S. women let Norway dictate the game.

"We played afraid and lost the game 1-0, and Norway took away our title as World Cup champions," Mia said. "On that day, they were clearly the better team. They were mentally tough and we weren't."

The jubilant Norwegian women celebrated with a victory conga line. The U.S. women watched through tear-stained eyes.

"It was easily the longest 10 minutes of my life, and I can assure you I haven't forgotten it because none of us looked away," Mia recalled. "We swore we'd never feel that way again and that the next time we met, it would be us in a pile of happy, sweaty bodies at the final whistle."

Because of Norway's victory, the U.S. women came in third in the 1995 World Cup. They left Sweden with bronze medals, but they wanted gold. They vowed to win back their title as world champions. They had less than 12 months before the 1996 Olympics.

New Role for Mia

Mia came away from the 1995 World Cup with the Most Valuable Player Award. She had proven herself as a player of remarkable all-around talent, switching positions from

Mia holds up her Most Valuable Player Award at the 1995 World Cup. (Getty Images)

forward to midfielder to goalie as needed. She had initiated most of the team's offensive drives. Before one of her two goals, she had made a spectacular 60-yard run down the field. Mia was beginning to eclipse Michelle Akers in public popularity.

A dazzling player, Mia was also a modest and well-spoken ambassador for women's soccer. She was quiet and shy everywhere but on the soccer field. Young fans loved to read articles about Mia. In July 1995, *Sports Illustrated for Kids* ended a story about Mia with a list of her favorite things. Her favorite color: green. Her favorite food: Italian. Her favorite TV show: *Seinfeld*.

After soccer, golf was Mia's favorite sport. She played nine holes of golf once a week. Golf taught her patience. Her secret ambition was to someday play on the women's professional golf tour.

But, compared to soccer, golf didn't stand a chance with Mia. Golf was a solo sport. And shy Mia preferred being surrounded by her teammates. In January of 1996, Mia and her teammates headed off to Florida to train for the Olympic games. Their 1991 World Cup victory had gone virtually unnoticed, and they had failed to bring home a victory at the 1995 World Cup. Now they had a chance to finally put women's soccer on the map.

7

OLYMPIC GOLD

Mia couldn't wait for the 1996 Olympics. "This is incredible for me," she told a reporter. "I grew up on the Olympics, watching the Olympic Games. I distinctly remember 1984, sitting down with my family and cheering all the greats on. Mary Lou Retton. Jackie Joyner-Kersee. My heroes and idols."

In the months leading up to the Olympic games Mia gained new visibility. Nike displayed pictures of the ponytailed soccer player in stores around the nation. Mia was truly becoming the face of women's soccer.

Preparing for Atlanta

Despite Mia's increasing fame, the team always came first for her. Determined to avenge their loss from the previous year, Mia and her teammates trained hard at their camp in Florida from January until the games began in July.

They increased their fitness regimen so they would be an even more powerful force.

DiCicco developed a new two-pronged strategy. First, he worked with the players to develop a sophisticated defensive strategy so the team could keep the ball in possession. Then he brought back the scrappy, offensive drive that had always made the team winners. He used a grant from the Olympic Games Committee to hire a sports psychologist.

Sports psychologist Colleen Hacker worked to develop the "slight edge" that separated first-place from second-place winners. She developed team exercises to develop trust and competitive cooperation. In one exercise, players led their blindfolded partners down a 600-foot cliff. For Mia and her teammates, knowing they could count on each other in such high-risk situations built a bond that was unbreakable. Hacker also gave the team its mantra for the 1996 Olympics: "Team before I."

As the "face of women's soccer," Mia received many endorsement offers, including one from Nike. (Landov)

The team became more cohesive than ever. Mia and her teammates trained hard but also found time to relax. They hit the malls and nightspots of Orlando. They played card games for Oreo cookies. They watched movies together.

Mia wanted one thing more than anything else: To win. A bronze medal wasn't enough. She wanted Olympic gold.

"I've worked too hard and too long to let anything stand in the way of my goals," she said. "I will not let my team down and I will not let myself down. I'm going to break myself in half to make sure it happens."

Olympic Games

Olympic fever swept the United States in the summer of 1996. Although the Olympics were held in Atlanta, Georgia, some events took place elsewhere because of limited space. Twenty-five thousand fans—the most ever to watch a women's soccer game in the United States—flocked to Orlando, Florida, to watch the U.S. women play their first match against Denmark in scorching heat. The temperature on the field soared to over 100 degrees.

Mia played like she was immune to the heat. While running full speed, she blasted in one goal from 12 yards away. She got by defenders by faking right, faking left, and then passing off to her teammate Tiffeny Milbrett. Every time Mia got the ball she was dangerous. The U.S. team beat Denmark 3-0. Media from around the world compared Mia to the great Brazilian soccer player Pelé in her combination of speed, power, and grace.

The next game pitted the U.S. team against the tough Swedish team. The Swedes went in determined to hold Mia back. Whenever she went after a loose ball, they knocked her down. Six times they pushed her down. Six times she got back up. Then, after the seventh time, Mia could no longer stand. She crawled off the field with a badly sprained ankle. The U.S. team still won 2-1.

Mia's ankle was so sore she could not play in the game against China on July 25 that ended in a 0-0 tie. Next, the U.S. faced archrival Norway in the semifinals. Mia wanted to get back the World Cup championship Norway had robbed them of the year before. She had her ankle heavily bandaged and convinced DiCicco to put her in.

Like Sweden, Norway focused its defense on Mia. Once again, players knocked her down repeatedly. Finally, officials called a foul on Norway for roughing up Mia. The U.S won a penalty kick. Michelle Akers, who was still a powerful shooter despite her chronic fatigue syndrome, shot the ball like a missile into the net. The U.S. won the game 2-1.

Mia was overjoyed. The Americans were going on to the finals. If they beat China, they'd win the Olympics.

Final Game

On August 1, 1996, the U.S. team played its final game against China at Sanford Stadium in Athens, Georgia. Some 76,000 spectators crowded into the stadium—the largest crowd ever assembled to watch a women's soccer game. Fans bore signs like "I Love Hamm" and "Hamm is Good." The National Team had come a long way from its days of playing in anonymity.

Mia looked into the crowd and saw her entire family. Her big brother Garrett was there despite the progression of his aplastic anemia. He was weak and could no longer work. Still, he couldn't turn down a chance to see his little sister compete in the Olympics.

After being awed by the crowd, Mia and her teammates got down to work. Mia's ankle still hurt, but she pushed past her pain to launch two spectacular offensive attacks. In the first, she and Kristine Lilly showed the bond they had developed since teenagers. Lilly picked up the ball and dribbled down the left side of the field. Mia raced down the right flank and angled toward the center. Lilly passed the ball right to Mia's foot. Mia kicked the ball low and hard to the corner to the net.

The spectators went crazy. "USA! USA!" they chanted.

But China's goalkeeper flicked away the ball with her hand, blocking the goal.

The U.S. players kept their cool. Mia knew that even if she didn't score, one of her teammates would come through. She was right. Shannon MacMillan pounced on the rebound for an easy goal.

Then the Chinese scored. At halftime, the score was tied 1-1. Mia's ankle throbbed, and she worried that by not playing at her best, she might be hurting the team. She asked a teammate if she should take herself out of the game. The teammate told her to stay in. The team needed her. Even if she weren't playing at 100 percent, Chinese defenders would swarm all around her so another American could get free.

Mia still wasn't convinced. She asked several other teammates if she should stay in. The vote was unanimous. Everyone wanted her to play.

In the second half, Mia set up a play that resulted in the winning goal. She passed the ball to Joy Fawcett who, in turn, kicked it to Tiffeny Milbrett, who made the goal. The U.S. led 2-1.

Then, with only a minute left, Mia's ankle gave out. Veteran player Carin Gabarra finished up the game for her. When the final whistle blew, the team burst onto the field in a frenzy of hugs and screams. Mia's ankle was too sore for her to join her teammates in their victory lap around the field. But, as soon as they finished, they crowded around her. Then they headed to the locker room to change into their sweats for the medal ceremony.

Mia limped onto the podium to the deafening chant of "USA! USA!" She thought about how far the team had come as a result of its hard work and persistence. A band played the "Star Spangled Banner." Each player was awarded the universal symbol of excellence: the Olympic gold medal.

The American women had once again made history. Now, five years after their historic World Cup victory, they had won the first-ever Olympic gold medal for women's soccer.

Reporters crowded around Mia, the team's leading scorer. They saw her as the team's star. She, however, did not see herself that way. She characteristically downplayed her own accomplishments to focus on those of the team.

"This team is incredible," she said. "We all believed in each other and this day. From the beginning this has been an entire team effort."

Mia knew that the victory would give women every-where a boost. "With everyone embracing the women in these Olympic Games, we see it's all right [for women] to be successful," Mia told *People* magazine. "You gotta work for it, but the opportunities are there, and that's a won-derful feeling."

New Heights

After the Olympics, Mia's star rose to new heights. Endorsement offers poured in from Pert Plus, Power Bar,

Pepsi, and Earth Grain breads. Every time someone made her an offer, Mia's reaction was, "Why me?" Her teammates persuaded her that the exposure would be good for soccer.

The media also clamored for her attention. Reporters interviewed her. Magazines clamored for interviews. David Letterman asked her to appear on his TV show. Mia used each opportunity as a chance to sell the game.

In 1997, *People* magazine chose Mia as one of its 50 Most Beautiful People. The article detailed Mia's lack of vanity. She wasn't one to spend $10,000 on beauty products. Her husband said that she didn't spend much time in front of the mirror. Her real passion was playing soccer. Afterwards, soccer star Pelé said her real beauty was that she played a beautiful game.

Mia looked at the publicity as good for soccer, but a bit embarrassing for herself. Fans admired her for her talent and humility. Girls wrote her letters, called out her name and crowded around her for autographs.

Mia patiently autographed ticket stubs, balls, T-shirts, even the foreheads of awestruck fans. She wanted fans to feel a connection with players. She wanted girls to have the kind of female role models she had lacked growing up. She wanted them to know they could be anything they wanted to be.

Mia told a reporter from the *Chicago Tribune* that she was a lot like her young fans. She, too, worried about how she was as a friend and a sister. Was she doing enough? Was she living up to her responsibilities? Sometimes she, too, felt frustrated and insecure. She needed to work on her confidence every day.

"It takes a constant nurturing," she explained. Competing at a high level required that kind of investment. Confidence needed to be remade every day like a bed.

"Someone tried to tell me that Michael Jordan doesn't have confidence problems," Mia told author Jere Longman. "He's probably very selective about who he shares it with."

Garrett

When Mia spoke to groups of people, she often passed out information about her brother Garrett's disease, aplastic anemia. She raised $50,000 for his care through a benefit soccer game.

Garrett was gravely ill. In 1996, a doctor told the family that his only hope of survival was a bone-marrow transplant. Mia would have gladly donated her own bone marrow, but, because Garrett was adopted, she wasn't a match. She used her celebrity to urge people to have a simple blood test done for bone marrow screening. Finally, on Valentine's Day of 1997, Garrett got the bone marrow transplant he needed.

At first, the operation seemed successful. For a time, it looked like Garrett might recover. But then, two months later, his immune system failed. He contracted an infection that attacked his brain. Mia watched her brother's eyes open for a second. She called out to him, but then he was gone.

Garrett Hamm died in April of 1997. He was 28 years old. He left behind a wife and son.

"Garrett was, and always will be, my inspiration," Mia said. "I learned so much through him about perseverance, about grace, about dignity."

Her loss gave her a new sense of purpose in life. She decided to use her celebrity for a higher good. Shortly after her brother's death, she organized the Garrett Game, an annual fund-raising event played by her U.S. National teammates and top college players to raise money for bone-marrow disease research.

And, with her teammates' support, she rededicated herself to soccer. Hard as it was, she knew that Garrett would have wanted her to keep playing. That was their bond.

Back in the Game

Mia's first game back was on a rainy day in Milwaukee. The U.S. National Team was playing South Korea. All of Mia's teammates wore black armbands in Garrett's memory.

"The game started, and something amazing happened that I'll remember forever," Mia later wrote. "Just thirty seconds into the match, the ball popped loose in front of the goal and I whacked it into the net. All the emotion from the fans and my teammates and from my ordeal rushed in at once. It was truly an overwhelming experience."

Mia ran toward the stands to celebrate her goal, then slid into a puddle. Her soggy teammates piled on top of her.

Mia was back in top form. She had proven her mental toughness. From now on, she knew that she could overcome even the most tragic of events if she put her mind to it and accepted help from others.

Top Scorer

Mia was clearly on a roll. From 1995 on, she led the U.S. National Team in scoring (19 goals and 18 assists in 1995; nine goals and 18 assists in 1996, and 18 goals and six assists in 1997). In 1998, she had her best year yet, racking up 20 goals and 20 assists. For an unprecedented fifth year in a row, she was named the U.S. Soccer Federation's Female Athlete of the Year.

In 1998, the U.S. competed in the Goodwill Games against the three tough teams of Denmark, China, and Norway. In the final game against China, Mia scored both goals to lead the U.S. to a 2-0 victory. After the game, Coach DiCicco praised Mia for turning in a "Michael Jordan-like performance."

Mia, meanwhile, was close to breaking soccer records. Only two soccer players—male or female—in the world had ever scored more than 100 goals. Elisabetta Vignotto of Italy, a soccer star in the 1970s and 1980s, held the world record of 107 career goals but was long retired. Carolina Morace, another retired player from Italy, had scored 105 career goals. On Friday, September 18, 1998, Mia became the third soccer player in the world to ever notch 100.

The U.S. National Team was competing against Russia before a sellout crowd in Rochester, New York. With the U.S. team leading 2-0, Hamm ripped the ball into the left side of the net, sending the crowd into a frenzy. The U.S. bench emptied onto the field to mob Mia. After the game Mia gave her teammates credit for the goal. "I wouldn't have scored any goals without them, and it's a credit to this team that we can have moments like this," she said.

Coach DiCicco praised Mia not only for her 100th career goal but also for her strength as a team player. "I was delighted that Mia got her 100th goal, but I was just as proud of her on the first goal, when she could have shot but found an open player in better position to score," he said. "Her team goals are always in front of her personal goals."

Indeed, Mia used the occasion to praise veteran player Michelle Akers, who was battling chronic fatigue syndrome. "Because of what Michelle has done for women's soccer, I wish she had reached one hundred before me, but of course that has never stopped me from scoring as many goals as I can," Mia said.

In her autobiography, Mia looked back on scoring her 100th goal with a typical mixture of embarrassment and pride. Yes, she was embarrassed by all the applause at the time. But, no, she couldn't take such moments for granted. "When my career is over, I'm sure I'll look back on that night with pride and nostalgia," she wrote.

8

WORLD CUP GLORY

Mia and her teammates spent the winter and spring of 1999 getting ready for the World Cup. They played an ambitious exhibition schedule to drum up interest in the event, since it would be the ultimate test of the popularity of non-Olympic women's sports in the United States. After the U.S. National Team's victory in the 1996 Olympics, people were more interested in women's soccer than ever before.

Given her increasing popularity, Mia was expected not only to lead her team to victory but also to fill stadiums, endorse products, give interviews, serve as a role model and bring her sport to the next level. Everywhere she went fans and reporters clamored for her attention.

Mia gladly accepted responsibility for promoting the World Cup, as long as the spotlight didn't shine on just her for too long. She didn't want the World Cup to turn into the "Mia Hamm Show." Her team-before-self attitude prevented potential jealousies from developing among players.

Over the years, Mia and her teammates had supported each other through marriages, pregnancies, divorces and deaths in the family. They had literally grown up together. Roommates were switched at every stop to prevent cliques from forming. She and her teammates shared an extraordinary bond.

Then they faced a challenge that threatened to tear them apart.

Sexual Harassment Suit

In the summer of 1998, Mia's teammate Debbie Keller filed a sexual harassment lawsuit against coach Anson Dorrance. Keller accused Dorrance, her coach at the University of North Carolina from 1993 to 1996, of making unwanted romantic advances toward her and engaging in inappropriate conversations with the players. [In 2004, a settlement was reached whereby Dorrance agreed to participate in an annual sensitivity program and pay Keller $10,000 in damages.]

During the winter of 1999, the situation was potentially explosive. Eight of the team's national players had, at one time or another, played for Dorrance. When Keller was not invited to the World Cup training camp that winter, she felt like she was being punished for the lawsuit. She took steps to be reinstated, which ultimately proved unsuccessful. Players varied in their opinions about who was being wronged—Keller or Dorrance.

Mia stood by her former coach and mentor. She and 100 other Tar Heel players signed a letter of support for Dorrance, praising his professionalism and integrity. Other players, however, sided with Keller.

Coach DiCicco called a meeting to maintain team unity. He drew three circles on the blackboard representing personal feelings, the U.S. National Team, and the lawsuit. He urged the players not to let one circle bleed into another. Sports psychologist Colleen Hacker made herself available for personal counseling.

At the World Cup training camp, Mia was assigned to room with a teammate who sympathized with Keller. One day, over ice cream, they discussed their feelings about the lawsuit and decided not to let it interfere with their bond to each other. The team came first. Dividing into factions would destroy the team.

For Mia, the team's reaction to the lawsuit showed how committed the players were to maintaining unity. They wouldn't let anything stand in the way of winning the World Cup.

Scoring Slump

Pressure on Mia mounted during the winter and spring of 1999. The world record for career goals scored was well within her grasp. Meanwhile, reporters and sponsors clamored for her attention. Everyone expected her to lead the team to victory. Mia felt the pressure.

For three months, she went without scoring a single goal. Reporters wrote about her scoring slump. The more Mia read the articles, the more her confidence plummeted.

One day she went into coach DiCicco's office and burst into tears. She told him she wanted to do things perfectly. She felt she had lost her step. He patiently told her that she hadn't. Her game just needed a little tune-up, not a complete overhaul. She needed to stop putting so much pressure on herself. Sports psychologist Colleen Hacker gave her a quote to build her confidence. "Perfect confidence is granted to the less talented as a consolation prize," it said.

Mia also turned to friends and teammates for advice. She called Red Sox shortstop Nomar Garciaparra, who had befriended the team the year before. He told her to go out and play for her love of the game.

Finally, on May 2, 1999, in Atlanta, Mia broke her eight-game scoreless streak in a game against Japan. The 20-yard blast was number 106 of her international career. Mia felt a gigantic sense of relief.

Then, in a game against Brazil on May 22, 1999, she scored record-breaking goal number 108. Mia now held the world record for most goals.

Another player might have basked in the glory, but not Mia. In a conference call with reporters, she described the play as "very reflective of our team, with lots of one-touch plays. I was fortunate to be at the end of it and knock it in."

Reporters kept asking her the dreaded question: "How does it feel to be the best woman soccer player in the world?" She always denied that she was. She was still trying to live up to the standards set by her teammates.

"Ask me that question when I can dominate on both offense and defense like [teammate] Kristine Lilly does," she'd reply. "Ask me when I can head a ball like Tisha Venturini, defend as well as Joy Fawcett, play an all-around game like Julie Foudy."

The Mia Hamm Foundation

On May 20, 1999, Mia announced the creation of a foundation to raise funds for two causes close to her heart: bone-marrow transplants and women's sports. Her interest in bone-marrow disease stemmed from her brother's illness, while her own positive experiences as a female athlete made her want to create more opportunities for young women in sports.

"Separately, these two issues have had a profound effect upon me as an individual and I am committed to raising funds and awareness for them," she said in a press release. "My goal is to leave a positive and lasting legacy in the research of bone marrow diseases and for every female athlete to have the opportunity to play the sports they love."

The foundation grew out of Mia's longstanding commitment to helping others, which came from her parents' strong community-service values. The foundation continued the annual Garrett Game and allowed Mia to expand her charitable efforts. She added a second major fundraiser: a golf tournament that attracted such notables as Olympian Marion Jones and NFL quarterback Doug Flutie. The foundation went to work sponsoring a national bone-marrow drive, kicked off a girls' mentoring program and provided grants to worthy organizations.

Kids began sending Mia money for the foundation. "You get kids that write and say, 'I heard you had a foundation' and they send you $10," she said. "It's so great."

Corporate sponsors Nike, Mattel, and Gatorade provided the financial backing for the foundation. In early June, Nike named a building in Mia's honor in its headquarters in Oregon. Mia's family and teammates joined her for the dedication ceremony. To further honor Mia, Nike agreed to stamp Garrett's initials, GJH, on the sole of each pair of its M-9 line of soccer shoes.

Gearing Up for the World Cup

To get ready for opening day of the World Cup, Mia and her teammates trained for a week in New Jersey. Sports psychologist Colleen Hacker had made motivational videos for each player to watch individually and left inspirational quotes for the players every day. The videos, each choreographed to the music of the player's choice, became group entertainment. Each night the team watched a few videos leading up to opening game.

Before the opening game on June 19, 1999, Mia and her teammates painted their fingernails and toenails red, white, and blue, as was their tradition before big games. They had an impromptu dance party in the hall of their hotel. They were fired up and ready to go.

When the team arrived at Giants Stadium in New Jersey, they found a roaring crowd of 78,000 fans. "Girls rule!" was the battle cry of the day. Mia thought about how far the team had come in the past decade. During the warm-ups, she and her teammates hugged each other.

"It was like we had achieved something we had worked for our whole lives, and the game hadn't even started yet!" Mia later wrote.

In the first game of the tournament, the United States faced off against Denmark. The game got off to a slow start. Then Mia raced downfield and caught a long pass about 15 yards from the net. The Danish defender tried to intercept the ball. But Mia faked her out. First she shifted left, then right. As the defender moved the wrong way, Mia shuffled the ball to her left foot. Mia powered a booming left-footed shot into the goal. The U.S. team won the match 3-0.

Next, the U.S. faced Nigeria. Once again, Mia blasted in a goal. The U.S. team beat Nigeria 7-0. Then, as the U.S. rolled into the quarterfinals and semifinals, Mia's scoring stopped. One reporter wrote that Mia was never a "big game overachiever." Fans wondered if something was wrong with their favorite player.

Mia maintained all along that she was just one of 20 exceptional players. She didn't need to score all the goals. Her teammates could also step up to the task, leaving her free to contribute in other ways. In the semifinals against Brazil, a foul against Mia led to a penalty kick for Michelle Akers. Still, people were talking. Why had Mia gone for four games without scoring a goal?

"Offensively, people say I haven't been as consistent," Mia told a reporter. "But I thought the German game was one of my better defensive games. I'm O.K. with the way things are going. I need to stay positive and keep motivated for Saturday."

World Cup Hoopla

As the final game approached, World Cup Fever swept across America. The crowds were so huge that the players needed a four-motorcycle escort. One overzealous fan wouldn't let go in a high five, causing teammate Michelle Akers to suffer a shoulder injury. The players decided to keep signing autographs. They owed it to their fans. "Mia! Mia! Mia!" the crowds screeched. Reporters coined a new term for the phenomenon: "Mia-mania."

More than 90,000 fans jammed into the Rose Bowl in Pasadena, California, for the final game against China on July 10, 1999, making it the biggest event in the history of sports. A record 40 million people watched the game on TV. President Clinton sat in a skybox at the edge of his seat.

On the field, the two teams battled each other. But no one scored. After two nail-biting overtime periods, the score was still 0-0. The game would be decided by penalty kicks. Each team would name five players to alternate kicking the ball from 12 yards away from the goal.

Assistant coach Lauren Gregg chose Mia as one of the five. Mia, however, had always struggled with penalty kicks. She worried that if she missed the kick, she'd cost her team the game. The pressure was enormous. She asked teammate Shannon MacMillan if she'd take the kick for her. MacMillan said she would.

Mia tried to talk Gregg into giving the kick to MacMillan. The assistant coach refused. She told Mia firmly that the roster was already made. Mia needed to take the kick.

The coach's confidence in her helped Mia decide to take the kick. She'd be kicking fourth.

The team gathered in a football huddle right before the shootout. Despite her nervousness, Mia told her teammates, "We deserve to be here. We're not going to lose this now." Later, she told author Jere Longman that she said those words as much to convince herself as to rally her teammates.

The tension mounted. Both teams made their first two kicks. Then American goalkeeper Briana Scurry made a spectacular save. The U.S. led by one in the shootout. To maintain her team's lead, Mia needed to make her kick.

Mia approached the ball, trying to summon up a type of confidence bordering on arrogance. She heard the excitement of the crowd. Then all the noise faded away, and her instincts took over. She booted a low, hard shot to the left of the goalkeeper. The shot was good.

Mia pumped her fist and yelled "Yeah!" Then she ran back and collapsed into a teammate's arms. She had confronted her fear and pulled through for the team.

Teammate Brandi Chastain made the final shot. The U.S. team had once again won the World Cup.

Celebration

After the game, Mia wept and hugged her teammates. They got their medals on stage and headed into a packed locker room. President Clinton congratulated the team for making the country proud. During the post-game press conference, Mia told journalists how grateful she was to her family and teammates.

A little while later, Mia collapsed on the locker room floor. She had given everything to the game. Her body had given out. The medical staff pumped three liters of fluids into her. She was physically and emotionally exhausted. She slept for nearly 12 hours. When she woke up, she realized she had missed the team's victory party.

The next day, she and her teammates embarked on a whirlwind post-victory celebratory tour, making stops along the way at Disneyland, the *Late Show* with David Letterman, and a WNBA All-Stars game. In New York City, Mia met her hero, track legend Jackie Joyner-Kersee, on the set of *Good Morning America*. That week, the World Cup made the covers of *People, Newsweek, Time,* and *Sports Illustrated*.

The next Sunday, the team gathered at the White House for a special ceremony with the president and first lady. Then they flew to Cape Canaveral to watch the first shuttle flight commanded by a woman.

Mia and her teammates became America's new heroes. The American women showed a passion for their sport, a sense of responsibility to their fans, and a commitment to each other. They showed Americans that their daughters, too, might someday go from playing amateur soccer to winning a world championship. They captured the hearts of America.

Role Model

Mia used her fame as an opportunity to serve as a role model. In 1999 she published her book, *Go for the Goal: A Champion's Guide to Winning in Soccer and Life.*

The book is part autobiography, part soccer manual, and part self-help book. Written with her young fans in mind, the book extols the virtues of teamwork, competition, confidence, hard work, and the pure joy of kicking a soccer ball.

"I firmly believe that if you pursue what you love, you will find happiness," she wrote. "We all know that the pursuit will be filled with its share of hardships and struggles, but if I can follow my life's passion despite all the changes in school, cities and friends of my childhood, so can you."

Mia also gave magazine interviews about being a role model. In an article in *USA Weekend* magazine, she said that while growing up team sports gave her a framework for meeting new people, confidence, self-esteem, time management, discipline, and motivation. She added that soccer is like life because, "You get out of it exactly what you put in it." Soccer, like life, sometimes seemed unfair.

Mia signs autographs for some of her fans. (Associated Press)

You could outshoot another team but still lose. The trick was to persevere.

In an article in *Sports Illustrated for Kids,* she said that sports could help girls grow into confident women. "Have fun, work hard, and never give up!" she said. "Sports can teach you many of life's most important lessons. But sports should always be fun."

9

A LEAGUE OF
THEIR OWN

With the nation abuzz from the World Cup victory, Mia and her teammates set out to build on their success. They knew the time was right for a professional league like the WNBA (Women's National Basketball Association) to create more opportunities for post-collegiate players. To keep up the momentum, they organized their own World Cup victory tour, a series of indoor games scheduled for October through December 1999.

But plans did not go as smoothly as expected. Officials at the U.S. Soccer Federation reacted angrily to news that the team had arranged its own victory tour backed by an outside marketing group. Each player would be earning about $100,000 for her participation. The U.S. Soccer Federation threatened to sue the team. Finally, the Federation agreed to let the tour proceed.

Bad feelings lingered, however. The U.S. Soccer Federation put off negotiating a new contract with the team.

Equal Pay

Mia wanted future generations of women to be able to earn a salary from playing soccer. For years, the Federation had paid members of the Women's National Team lower salaries than their male counterparts. In 1999, members of the women's team earned about $40,000 each for the World Cup's six-month residency camp. Meanwhile, the men earned about $135,000 each.

Mia was less dependent on her salary than other members of the team because she brought in millions of dollars in endorsement fees. But she wanted salaries to be fair for her teammates and future generations of women. She stuck by her teammates during the tough contract negotiations. Together they boycotted a tournament in January of 2000 in Australia because a fair contract was nowhere in sight.

Finally, on February 1, 2000, the U.S. Soccer Federation agreed to a contract that would put the American women on equal terms with the American men. Each player would receive $2,000 per match in appearance fees, up from $150 per match, as well as a guarantee of $5,000 per month, up from $3,150.

New League

During the contract negotiations, Mia and her teammates raised the issue of a professional soccer league for women. The U.S. Soccer Federation proposed a plan linking the new league to Major League Soccer (MLS), the struggling men's professional league. The women, however, wanted it to be independent. Federation officials asked where they'd get the money.

Mia and her teammates turned to John Hendicks, the founder of the Discovery Channel and a supporter of women's soccer since the 1996 Olympics. He called his friends in the cable industry and raised $40 million.

Mia and her teammates were ecstatic. Their dream of a new professional soccer league for women was becoming a reality. The players named their new league the Women's United Soccer Association (WUSA). In August of 2000, the U.S. Soccer Federation sanctioned the new league.

"The league is everything we've fought for," Mia told *Sports Illustrated for Women*. The first game of the new Women's United Soccer Association would be in April 2001. But first, she and her teammates needed to get ready for the 2000 Olympics that September.

The 2000 Olympics

As the reigning world champions, the U.S. women went into the 2000 Olympics in Sydney, Australia, as the obvious favorites. In the opening match, Mia scored one of the team's two goals to defeat Norway 2-0. She also scored the game-winning goal in the team's semifinal match against Brazil. The Americans were going on to the finals. Mia and her teammates would be squaring off against archrival Norway, the team that had won the 1995 World Cup.

The game got off to a good start for the Americans. Then Norway edged ahead 2-1 in the second half. Mia and her teammates refused to give up. In the final minutes of regulation play, Mia assisted on Tiffeny Milbrett's second goal of the game. With the score tied at 2-2, the match went into overtime.

Whoever scored the next goal would win the Olympics. Mia was stunned when it turned out to be Norway. She fell to her knees and stared at the ground for a long time. The U.S. would be going home with silver, not gold. After the loss, reporters crowded around Mia.

"Tell me," a reporter asked her. "What's your message to all the little girls around America who see you as a role model?" For years, Mia had been asked the question after winning. Now she was being asked after losing.

"You know, we put so much pressure on kids—to win, to be first," she replied. True success, she thought, went beyond winning or losing the game. "It's about giving everything you have," she said. "That's success."

The U.S. Women's Soccer Team received their silver medals at the 2000 Olympics. (Getty Images)

Mia knew her team had played great soccer. After a soft cry in the locker room, she took it on herself to rally the troops. She went up to every teammate on the medal podium and said, "Hold your head high—and be proud."

Opening Day

After the Olympics, Mia and her teammates prepared themselves for the opening day of the Women's United Soccer Association on April 14, 2001. Mia and her 19 teammates were divided among eight teams. Mia became part of the Washington Freedom. Players from other countries also joined the league. Old rivals became teammates. Team-mates became competitors.

Mia tirelessly promoted the new league even though the task of spokesperson did not come easily to her. She was not a naturally chatty person. Still, she wanted to get out word about the league.

On April 14, 2001, the Washington Freedom played its opening game of the season to a crowd of 34,148 fans—more than twice as many as expected—at RFK Stadium in Washington, D.C. Mia played with a nagging shoulder injury. As the season progressed, the Washington Free-dom and Mia, herself, failed to live up to the public's expectations. She wasn't used to so much losing. The Washington Freedom tied for last place in the WUSA with a record of six wins, 12 losses, and three ties. In 19 games in 2001, Mia scored only six goals and three assists.

Observers said that Mia looked physically and mentally exhausted. She needed to juggle the needs of the league, her corporate clients, the media, and her fans.

Slump and Divorce

As the demands on Mia's time increased, injuries slowed her down. Reporters joked that "Mia" stood for "Missing in Action." She attributed her slump to a combination of physical, personal, and psychological factors. "They all play on one another," she told a reporter.

Mia and some teammates from the Washington Freedom
(Getty Images)

People began to wonder if Mia's extraordinary career was coming to a close. Had she passed her prime? Was it time to quit?

"I wasn't too happy as a person," she told the *New York Times*. "I kind of lost my passion for the game."

Mia's marriage, meanwhile, was floundering. She and her husband, Christiaan Corry, a Marine helicopter pilot, often spent weeks or months apart because of the demands of their separate careers. The couple separated in 2000. In July of 2001, Mia told a reporter that she had begun divorce proceedings with Corry. For Mia, athletic success had come at a personal cost: the breakdown of her marriage.

"Our career paths really never crossed," Mia said. "We were both committed to what we were doing . . . I know a lot of times I wasn't there for him, and that I regret."

Upswing

The year 2001 also had its bright spots. Mia got great satisfaction from her work with the foundation. At halftime at the 2001 Garrett Game, she brought together bone marrow donors and recipients for the first time. "It was clearly my most satisfying moment away from the field," she said.

Mia also took pride in her role as a pioneer in women's soccer. In 2001, FIFA, the international governing body for soccer, created its first Women's Player of the Year Award. Mia won the award for both 2001 and 2002.

In February of 2002, Mia underwent surgery on her knee. The four months of rehabilitation gave her a chance to step back and refocus. Mia got over her funk by focusing on the things she could control. She worked hard on rehabbing her knee. She leaned on family and friends for emotional support.

When she returned to the lineup in June, she felt rejuvenated. The Washington Freedom, which was on a losing streak, started winning games. Mia racked up more goals and assists per minute than any other player in the team. Her team came close to winning the championship. She was determined to lead the Washington Freedom to victory the following year.

10

RETIREMENT BECKONS

In the fall of 2002, Mia became engaged to baseball player Nomar Garciaparra. The two met in 1998 at a promotional event at Harvard. Later, *Sports Illustrated* recounted their meeting. They each took five kicks to entertain the fans. Mia made four, Nomar three.

"Thanks for throwing it," she told him.

"I had to let you win," replied Nomar.

Then, when Mia was in a slump in 1999, she dug out Nomar's phone number and called him for advice. Nomar had played soccer all through high school. He asked if her team was winning. She said it was. He asked if she was playing well outside of her scoring. She told him she was.

"Then you've got to just enjoy the game," he said. "You've got to stop worrying."

Mia and Nomar began dating after her divorce in 2001. Nomar was a star in his own right so he could shield Mia from the spotlight. In his years as a star shortstop for the Boston Red Sox, he had learned to live comfortably with his fame. He knew how to set limits. She could learn from him.

The two trained together during the off-season. They went to each other's charity events and games. Mia became a fixture behind home plate at Fenway Park. Fans liked seeing the two charitable, hardworking athletes together. Mia and Nomar planned to get married after the 2003 World Cup.

People noticed a change in Mia once she started dating Nomar. She seemed more playful and happy-go-lucky. In one interview, she joked about how she would not change her name to Hamm-Garciaparra, saying, "At my age I need the least wind-resistance from my jersey." In another interview, she talked about how she'd come to accept herself more. "To be honest with you, there were times I'd beat myself up," she said. She wanted to be like her teammates—more chatty and relaxed with the media. But then she realized she could not be like that. And she accepted it.

For years, reporters had written about Mia's intensity. She always seemed to have her "game face" on. But now she seemed to be enjoying herself more. She even looked more comfortable in the spotlight.

On May 14, 2003, Mia appeared on NBC's *Today* show as part of the program's "trading places" series. Mia switched jobs with news anchor Ann Curry, who, in turn, strapped on her soccer cleats to join the Washington Freedom for a day. Four years earlier, Mia might have balked at appearing on TV unless her teammates could come along.

Best WUSA Season

In the spring of 2003, Mia went into her third season of the WUSA feeling strong mentally and physically. For the first time in two years, she was free of injuries. Her per-

Mia and her husband, Nomar Garciaparra, kick a soccer ball at Boston's Fenway Park. (Associated Press)

sonal life was going well, too. And, when she was happy, she played her best soccer.

Fans often came up to her to thank her for all she'd done for women's soccer. True to form, Mia refused to take all the credit. "I might be the face, but I'm definitely not the brains to this whole thing," she told reporters.

In the 2003 WUSA season, she and teammate Abby Wambach topped the league in scoring, each racking up 11 goals and 11 assists. In August of 2003, the Washington Freedom won WUSA's top prize, the Founders Cup. Yet another of Mia's dreams had come true.

But the league's financial picture looked far from rosy. Corporate sponsors were cutting back. Mia and her teammates took salary cuts from $85,000 to $60,000 to keep the league alive.

End of the League

On September 15, 2003, the Women's United Soccer Association announced that it was suspending operations immediately. There was no money for a fourth season. Many sponsors had pulled out of the WUSA in response to a shaky economy and declining attendance.

"We're sad. We're all sad," Mia said in regard to these developments.

Mia could still play with the national league and earn money from endorsements. But she wanted to keep opportunities alive for the lesser-known players who depended on the league for their incomes.

Women's basketball had taken several tries before the WNBA got off the ground. So Mia and many others hope that women's soccer, too, will once again have a league of its own.

The 2003 World Cup

Mia wanted to pass on a love of soccer to future generations. She knew that her own playing career couldn't last forever. The 2003 World Cup—her fourth—would be her last. She planned to retire after the 2004 Olympics.

"For so long, the game has just been my entire life," she told the *Washington Times.* "And now it doesn't need to be, and that's wonderful . . . It's given me the structure from where I can step away from it."

Too often in the past, she had pushed herself so hard, she couldn't just take pleasure in the game. Now that she was older, she was beginning to feel more nostalgic about her experiences. She wanted to enjoy her final World Cup.

Her playing in 2003 showed a new level of versatility and confidence. She told reporters that the biggest challenge of her career was just trying to be a consistent player. Confidence, she said, helped players be more consistent by making their peaks and valleys less noticeable.

As the World Cup got underway in late September, Mia showed a new level of confidence. Her old self-doubt had faded. In the series opener, Mia assisted on all three goals against Sweden. Next, she scored two goals and one assist in a very physical game against Nigeria.

She was a different Mia from the one who didn't want to take a penalty kick in the 1999 World Cup. Now she wanted to take the kick. In the World Cup game against Nigeria, she nailed her shot to bring the U.S. to a 5-0 victory.

Perhaps even more revealing was the penalty kick Mia took in the quarterfinal game against Norway on October 1, 2003. This time she missed the shot.

"A while back [missing the shot] would have been a big deal for me, but we still had 25, 30 minutes to play to get one back, so it was just a matter of, 'All right, now I need to work for our team to make sure it doesn't cost us.'"

She did just that, leading her team to a 1-0 victory over Norway. The U.S. was going on to the semifinals.

On October 5, the U.S. faced off against Germany in the semifinals. Mia came close to scoring. But the German goaltender rebuffed her shot. The U.S. lost 3-0.

Mia was gracious in defeat. "Their goalkeeper was aggressive and made great plays," she told the Knight Ridder/Tribune News Service. "They are an exceptional team."

Wedding

Mia and Nomar wanted their wedding to be a private affair, not a media circus. The *Boston Herald* reported that their wedding invitations—adorned with hearts with Mia's number 9 inside one and Nomar's number 5 inside the other—came without the time or place of the nuptials. Mia invited all her teammates from the National Team and the Washington Freedom. Guests were given a phone number to call with a password to get the time and place of the wedding. The invitations also informed guests that there were to be no cell phones, cameras, video equipment, or autograph hunting at the festivities.

The media-shy couple tied the knot on November 22, 2003, in front of about 400 relatives and friends in California. Mia and Nomar turned down a number of offers from magazines to sell the wedding photos because they wanted the affair to be private.

Then the newlyweds set off to Hawaii for their honeymoon. When they got home, Mia started training for her next big event: the 2004 Olympics.

The Athens Olympics

In the winter of 2004, the U.S. team won a series of qualifying matches for the summer games. Also that winter, Mia signed a contract with HarperCollins Publishers for a picture book titled *Winners Never Quit,* about how she learned persistence from playing soccer with her siblings. In April of 2004, Mia and her teammates began four months of intensive training for the Olympics in their resident camp in Los Angeles.

In the months leading up to the Olympics, media coverage focused on Mia's looming retirement. Reporters asked if she was planning to become "the ultimate soccer mom." "I just want to be a mom," she replied. "Whether they play soccer or love music, I'll just be proud of them and support them." At the end of July, Nomar was traded from the Boston Red Sox to the Chicago Cubs. Mia and her teammates showed their loyalty to Nomar by replacing their Red Sox hats with the blue caps of the Chicago Cubs.

In early August, Mia and her teammates flew to Athens, Greece, for the 2004 Olympics. It was the last Olympics Mia would be playing with her old teammates Kristine Lilly, Julie Foudy, Joy Fawcett, and Brandi Chastain. The media dubbed them the Fab Five. These veterans had helped put women's soccer on the map. Younger members of the team wanted to win a gold medal so the veterans could go out in a blaze of glory.

Mia entered the Olympics looking strong and confident. At 32, she was an "old lady" in international soccer. Yet she still had top-notch skills. In the opening game against Greece on August 11, she scored one goal and assisted on another to give the Americans a 2-0 victory.

The team moved on to the quarterfinals and then the semifinals. On August 24, Mia and her teammates faced off against the world-champion German team in the semifinals. Before the game got underway, coach April Heinrichs gave an emotional locker room speech. "It's fitting for these players to go out on top," Henrichs said about the veterans. "We owe it to them."

Both teams played hard. With the score tied 1-1 in overtime, Mia moved in from the right flank and shot the ball to 19-year-old Heather O'Reilly, who scored the winning goal. When Mia kicked the ball to O'Reilly, it was like she was passing the torch to the next generation. Many of the younger members of the team had grown up with Mia's poster on their wall. She had inspired a whole generation of girls to kick a soccer ball. Through her, they had learned that female athletes could be both tough and feminine.

On August 26, the United States faced Brazil in the gold-medal match. The Brazilian players were younger and faster than the American women. But Mia and her teammates never gave up. In overtime, the Americans won 2-1. They were once again world champions.

Even though Mia had made no spectacular plays during the game, she was the one everyone ran to. She was still the face of women's soccer. Mia and her teammates held hands on the medal stand and sang the national anthem.

During the gold-medal ceremony, Mia's eyes welled up with tears. Her fellow Olympians chose her to carry the flag in the closing ceremonies of the Olympics. She was the first U.S. soccer player ever to do so.

In her 17-year-long career, Mia had scored a world-record 153 goals and helped the United States women's team win two World Cups and two Olympic gold medals. She had spent more than half her life in soccer, sharing both the joys and sorrows with her teammates. She had overcome scoring droughts and confidence problems. In the process, she told her young fans, she never forgot that "There's no 'me' in 'Mia.'" For her, the team always came first.

"It's been a wonderful journey that has let me experience a whole variety of emotions," Mia said as her extraordinary career came to a close. "It has taught me a lot about life and about the value of friendship."

TIME LINE

1972   Born in Selma, Alabama, on March 17 to Bill, an Air Force pilot, and Stephanie, a former ballerina; Congress passes Title IX mandating gender equality in sports

1973   Moves to Italy where father is stationed; kicks her first soccer ball

1977   Plays in Peewee Soccer League in Wichita, Texas

1982   Watches Men's World Cup broadcast with family

1987   Becomes youngest woman to ever play with the U.S. National Team at age 15

1991   Plays in first-ever Women's World Cup; U.S. team's victory largely ignored by media

1994   Graduates from the University of North Carolina with degree in political science; named U.S. Soccer's

Female Athlete of the Year for the first of a record five years in a row; marries Christiaan Corry on December 17

1995   Named National Team's Most Valuable Player for 1995 World Cup in which she played a variety of positions, including goalkeeper

1996   Wins gold medal at 1996 Olympics

1997   Mourns death of brother Garrett; organizes Garrett Game; named as one of *People* magazine's 50 Most Beautiful People

1998   Becomes first U.S. player to score 100 goals in career

1999   Breaks world record for career goals scored—male or female—in soccer when she scores her 108th goal on May 22; leads U.S. to World Championship at Women's World Cup in July; founds Mia Hamm Foundation; publishes *Go for the Goal: A Champion's Guide to Winning in Soccer and Life*

2000   Wins silver medal at 2000 Olympics; helps teammates win salary equal to Men's National Team; helps found the Women's United Soccer Association (WUSA)

2001   Becomes founding member of the WUSA's
Washington Freedom; divorces husband Christiaan
Corry; named first FIFA Women's Player of the Year

2002   Recuperates from knee surgery; tops WUSA in goals
and assists scored per minute

2003   Leads Washington Freedom to Founders Cup championship shortly before WUSA suspends operations;
marries baseball player Nomar Garciaparra on
November 22 in California

2004   Announces plans to retire; publishes children's picture book *Winners Never Quit*; helps team win gold
medal at Olympics on August 26 in Athens, Greece;
chosen by fellow athletes to carry the American
flag in closing ceremonies of Olympics August 29

HOW TO BECOME A PROFESSIONAL ATHLETE

THE JOB

Unlike amateur athletes who play or compete in amateur circles for titles or trophies only, professional athletic teams compete against one another to win titles, championships, and series. Team members are paid salaries and bonuses for their work.

The athletic performances of individual teams are evaluated according to the nature and rules of each specific sport: Usually the winning team compiles the highest score, as in football, basketball, and soccer. Competitions are organized by local, regional, national, and international organizations and associations, whose primary functions are to promote the sport and sponsor competitive events. Within a professional sport there are usually different levels of competition based on age, ability, and gender. There are often different designations and divisions within one sport. Professional baseball, for example, is made up of the two major leagues (American and National) each made up of three divisions, East, Central, and West, and the minor leagues (Single-A, Double-A, Triple-A). All of these teams are considered professional because the players are compensated for their work, but the financial rewards are the greatest in the major leagues.

Whatever the team sport, most team members specialize in a specific area of the game. In gymnastics, for example, the entire six-member team trains on all of the gymnastic apparatuses—balance beam, uneven bars, vault, and floor exercise—but usually each of the six gymnasts excels in only one or two areas. Those gymnasts who do excel in all four events are likely to do well in the individual, all-around title, which is a part of the team competition. Team members in football, basketball, baseball, soccer, and hockey all assume different positions, some of which change depending on whether or not the team is trying to score a goal (offensive positions) or prevent the opposition from scoring one (defensive positions). During team practices, athletes focus on their specific role in a game, whether that is defensive, offensive, or both. For example, a pitcher will spend some time running bases and throwing to other positions, but the majority of his or her time will most likely be spent practicing pitching.

Professional teams train for most of the year, but unlike athletes in individual sports, the athletes who are members of a team usually have more of an off-season. Professional athletes' training programs differ according to the season. Following an off-season, most team sports have a training season in which they begin to increase the intensity of their workouts after a period of relative inactivity, in order to develop or maintain strength, cardiovascular ability, flexibility, endurance, speed, and quickness, as well as to focus on technique and control. During the season the team coach, physician, trainers, and physical therapists organize specific routines, programs, or exercises to target game skills as well as individual athletic weaknesses, whether skill-related or from injury.

These workouts also vary according to the difficulty of the game schedule. During a playoff or championship series, the coach and athletic staff realize that a rigorous workout in between games might tax the athletes' strength, stamina, or even mental preparedness, jeopardizing the outcome of the next game. Instead, the coach might prescribe a mild workout followed by intensive stretching. In addition to stretching and exercising the specific muscles used in any given sport, athletes concentrate on developing excellent eating and sleeping habits that will help them remain in top condition throughout the year. Abstaining from drinking alcoholic beverages during a season is a practice to which many professional athletes adhere.

The coaching or training staff often films the games and practices so that the team can benefit from watching their individual exploits, as well as its combined play. By watching their performances, team members can learn how to improve their techniques and strategies. It is common for professional teams to also study other teams' moves and strategies in order to determine a method of coping with the other teams' plays during a game.

REQUIREMENTS
High School

Most professional athletes demonstrate tremendous skill and interest in their sport well before high school. High school offers student athletes the opportunity to gain experience in the field in a structured and competitive environment. Under the guidance of a coach, you can begin developing suitable training programs and learn about health, nutrition, and conditioning issues.

High school also offers you the opportunity to experiment with a variety of sports and a variety of positions within a sport. Most junior varsity and some varsity high school teams allow you to try out different positions and begin to discover whether you have more of an aptitude for the defensive dives of a goalie or for the forwards' front-line action. High school coaches will help you learn to expand upon your strengths and abilities and develop yourself more fully as an athlete. High school is also an excellent time to begin developing the concentration powers, leadership skills, and good sportsmanship necessary for success on the field.

People who hope to become professional athletes should take a full load of high school courses including four years of English, math, and science, as well as health and physical education. A solid high school education will help ensure success in college (often the next step in becoming a professional athlete) and may help you earn a college athletic scholarship. A high school diploma will certainly give you something to fall back on if an injury, a change in career goals, or other circumstance prevents you from earning a living as an athlete.

Postsecondary Training

College is important for future professional athletes for several reasons. It provides the opportunity to gain skill and strength in your sport before you try to succeed in the pros, and it also offers you the chance of being observed by professional scouts.

Perhaps most important, a college education provides you with a valuable degree that you can use if you do not earn a living as a professional athlete or after your professional career ends. College athletes major in everything from communications to premed and enjoy careers as coaches, broadcasters, teachers, doctors, actors, and businesspeople, to name a few. As with high school sports, college athletes must maintain certain academic standards in order to be permitted to compete in intercollegiate play.

Other Requirements

If you want to be a professional athlete, you must be fully committed to succeeding. You must work almost nonstop to improve your conditioning and skills, and not give up when you do not succeed as quickly or as easily as you had hoped. And even then, because the competition is so fierce, the goal of earning a living as a professional athlete is still difficult to reach. For this reason, professional athletes must not get discouraged easily. They must have the self-confidence and ambition to keep working and keep trying. Professional athletes also must have a love for their sport that compels them to want to reach their fullest potential.

EXPLORING

Students interested in pursuing a career in professional sports should start playing that sport as much and as early as possible. Most junior high and high schools have well-established programs in the sports that are played at the professional level.

If a team sport does not exist in your school, that does not mean your chances of playing it have evaporated. Petition your school board to establish it as a school sport and set aside funds for it. In the meantime organize other students into a club team, scheduling practices and unofficial games. If the sport is a recognized team sport in the United States or Canada, contact the sport's professional organization for additional information. If anyone would have helpful tips for gaining recognition, the professional organization would. Also, try calling the local or state athletic board to see whether or not any other schools in your area recognize it as a team sport, and make a list of those teams and try scheduling exhibition games with them. Your goal is to show your school or school board that other students have a definite interest in the game and that other schools recognize it.

To determine if you really want to commit to pursuing a professional career in your team sport, talk to coaches, trainers, and any athletes who are currently pursuing a professional career. You can also contact professional organizations and associations for information on how to best prepare for a career in their sport. Sometimes there are specialized training programs available, and the best way to find out is to get in contact with the people whose job it is to promote the sport.

EMPLOYERS

Professional athletes are employed by private and public ownership groups throughout the United States and Canada. At the highest male professional level, there are 32 National Football League franchises, 30 Major League Baseball franchises, 29 National Basketball Association franchises, 30 National Hockey League franchises, and 10 Major League Soccer franchises. The Women's National Basketball Association has 16 franchises.

STARTING OUT

Most team sports have some official manner of establishing which teams acquire which players. Often this is referred to as a *draft,* although sometimes members of a professional team are chosen through a competition. Usually the draft occurs between the college and professional levels of the sport. The National Basketball Association (NBA), for example, has its NBA College Draft. During the draft the owners and managers of professional basketball teams choose players in an order based on the team's performance in the previous season. This means that the team with the worst record in the previous season has a greater chance of getting to choose first from the list of available players.

Furthermore, professional athletes must meet the requirements established by the organizing bodies of their respective sport. Sometimes this means meeting a physical requirement, such as age, height, and weight. Other times it means fulfilling a number of required stunts or participating in a certain number of competitions. Professional organizations usually arrange it so that athletes can build up their skills and level of play by participating in lower-level competitions. College sports, as mentioned before, are an excellent way to improve one's skills while pursuing an education.

ADVANCEMENT

Professional athletes in team sports advance in three ways: when their team advances, when they are traded to better teams, and when they negotiate better contracts. In all three instances, the individual team member who works and practices hard, and who gives his or her best performance in game after game, achieves this. Winning teams also receive a deluge of media attention that often creates celebrities out of individual players, which in turn provides these top players with opportunities for financially rewarding commercial endorsements.

Professional athletes are usually represented by *sports agents* in the behind-the-scenes deals that determine for which teams they will be playing and what they will be paid. These agents may also be involved with other key decisions involving commercial endorsements, personal income taxes, and financial investments of the athlete's revenues.

In the moves from high school athletics to collegiate athletics and from collegiate athletics to the pros, coaches and scouts are continually scouring the ranks of high school and college teams for new talent. They're most interested in the athletes who consistently deliver points or prevent the opposition from scoring. There is simply no substitute for success.

A college education, however, can prepare all athletes for the day when their bodies can no longer compete at the top level, whether because of age or an unforeseen injury. Every athlete should be prepared to move into another career, whether it is related to the world of sports or not.

Professional athletes do have other options, especially those who have graduated from a four-year college or university. Many go into some area of coaching, sports administration, management, or broadcasting. The professional athlete's unique insight and perspective can be a real asset in these careers. Other athletes simultaneously pursue other interests, some completely unrelated to their sport, such as education, business, social welfare, or the arts. Many continue to stay involved with the sport they have loved since childhood, coaching young children or volunteering with local school teams.

EARNINGS

Today professional athletes who are members of top-level teams earn hundreds of thousands of dollars in prize money at professional competitions. The top players or athletes in each sport earn as much or more in endorsements and advertising, usually for sports-related products and services, but increasingly for products or services completely unrelated to their sport. Such salaries and other incomes are not representative of the whole field of professional athletes but are only indicative of the fantastic revenues a few rare athletes with extraordinary talent can hope to earn. In 2003 athletes had median annual earnings of $45,780, according to the U.S. Department of Labor. The lowest paid 10 percent earned less than $13,310, and the highest paid 10 percent earned more than $145,600.

Perhaps the only caveat to the financial success of an elite athlete is the individual's character or personality. An athlete with a bad temper or who is prone to unsportsmanlike behavior may still be able to participate in team play, helping to win games and garner trophies, but he or she won't necessarily be able to cash in on the commercial endorsements. Advertisers are notoriously fickle about the spokespeople they choose to endorse products. Some athletes have lost million-dollar accounts because of their bad behavior on and off the court.

WORK ENVIRONMENT

Athletes compete in many different conditions, according to the setting of the sport (indoors or outdoors) and the rules of the organizing or governing bodies. Athletes who participate in football or soccer, for example, often compete in hot, rainy, or freezing conditions, but, at any point, organizing officials can call off the match or postpone competition until the weather improves.

Indoor events are less subject to cancellation. However, since it is in the best interests of an organization not to risk the athletes' health, any condition that might adversely affect the outcome of a competition is usually reason to cancel or postpone it. The coach or team physician, on the other hand, may withdraw an athlete from a game if that athlete is injured or ill. Nerves and fear are not good reasons to default on a competition, and part of ascending into the ranks of professional athletes means learning to cope with the anxiety that comes with competition. Some athletes, however, actually thrive on the nervous tension.

In order to reach the elite level of any sport, athletes must begin their careers early. Most professional athletes have been honing their skills since they were quite young. Athletes fit hours of practice time into an already full day. Many famous players practiced on their own before school, as well as for several hours after school during team practice. Competitions are often far from the young athlete's home, which means they must travel on a bus or in a van with the team and coaching staff. Sometimes young athletes are placed in special training programs far from their homes and parents. They live with other athletes training for the same sport or on the same team and only see their parents for holidays and vacations. The separation from a child's parents and family can be difficult. Often an athlete's family decides to move in order to be closer to the child's training facility.

The expenses of a sport can be overwhelming, as is the time an athlete must devote to practice and travel to and from competitions. Although most high school athletic programs pay for many expenses, if the athlete wants additional training or private coaching, the child's parents must come up with the extra money. Sometimes young athletes can get official sponsors or they might qualify for an athletic scholarship from the training program. In addition to specialized equipment and clothing, the athlete must sometimes pay for a coach, travel expenses, competition fees, and, depending on the sport, time at the facility or gym where he or she practices. Gymnasts, for example, train for years as individuals, and then compete for positions on national or international teams. Up until the time they are accepted (and usually during their participation in the team), these gymnasts must pay for their expenses—from coaching to travel to uniforms to room and board away from home.

Even with the years of hard work, practice, and financial sacrifice that most athletes and their families must endure, there is no guarantee that an athlete will achieve the rarest of the rare in the sports world—financial reward. An athlete needs to truly love the sport at which he or she excels and also have a nearly insatiable ambition and work ethic.

OUTLOOK

The outlook for professional athletes will vary depending on the sport, its popularity, and the number of positions open with professional teams. On the whole, the outlook for the field of professional sports is healthy, but the number of jobs will not increase dramatically. Some sports, however, may experience a rise in popularity, which may translate into greater opportunities for higher salaries, prize monies, and commercial endorsements.

TO LEARN MORE ABOUT PROFESSIONAL ATHLETES

BOOKS

Beckham, David, and Tom Watt. *Beckham: Both Feet on the Ground. An Autobiography.* New York: HarperCollins, 2003.

Coffey, Wayne. *Carl Lewis: The Triumph of Discipline.* Woodbridge, Conn.: Blackbirch Press, 1992.

Freedman, Russell. *Babe Didrikson Zaharias.* New York: Clarion, 1999.

Krull, Kathleen. *Lives of the Athletes: Thrills, Spills (And What the Neighbors Thought).* New York: Harcourt Brace, 1997.

Reyna, Claudio, and Mike Woitalla. *More Than Goals: The Journey from Backyard Games to World Cup Competition.* Champaign, Ill.: Human Kinetics, 2004.

Rudeen, Kenneth. *Jackie Robinson.* New York: HarperTrophy, 1996.

Stewart, Mark. *Tiger Woods: Driving Force.* Danbury, Conn.: Children's Press, 1998.

Updyke, Rosemary Kissinger. *Jim Thorpe, the Legend Remembered.* New York: Pelican, 1997.

ORGANIZATIONS AND WEBSITES

Young people who are interested in becoming professional athletes should contact the professional organizations for the sport in which they would like to compete, such as the National Hockey League, U.S. Tennis Association, the Professional Golfer's Association, or the National Bowling Association. Ask for information on requirements, training centers, coaches, and so on.

For a free brochure and information on the Junior Olympics and more, write to

Amateur Athletic Union
c/o The Walt Disney World Resort
P.O. Box 10000
Lake Buena Vista, FL 32830-1000
http://www.aausports.org

For additional information on athletics, contact

American Alliance for Health, Physical Education, Recreation, and Dance

1900 Association Drive

Reston, VA 20191

http://www.aahperd.org

Visit the U.S. Olympic Committee's website for the latest sporting news and information about upcoming Olympic competitions.

United States Olympic Committee

http://www.olympic-usa.org

The following website provides information about and links to women in all kinds of sports:

Women in Sports

http://www.makeithappen.com/wis/index.html

TO LEARN MORE ABOUT MIA HAMM

BOOKS

Adams, Sean. *Mia Hamm.* Sports Heroes and Legends. New York: Barnes and Noble Books, 2003.

Christopher, Matt. *On the Field with . . . Mia Hamm.* Boston: Little, Brown and Company, 1998.

Hamm, Mia. *Go for the Goal: A Champion's Guide to Winning in Soccer and Life.* New York: HarperCollins, 1999.

Longman, Jere. *The Girls of Summer: The U.S. Women's Soccer Team and How It Changed the World,* New York: HarperCollins, 2001.

Rutledge, Rachel. *Mia Hamm: Striking Superstar.* Brookfield, Conn.: Millbrook Press, 2000.

Smith, Lissa, editor. *Nike Is A Goddess: The History of Women in Sports.* New York: Atlantic Monthly Press, 1998.

Thomas, Marlo, and Friends. *The Right Words at the Right Time.* New York: Simon & Schuster, 2002.

MAGAZINES AND NEWSPAPERS

"Baseball Star Nomar Garciaparra Weds Soccer Great Mia Hamm in California," Associated Press, November 23, 2003.

"Fitting Farewell for America's Golden Girl," Yahoo! Sports, August 27, 2004.

"Golf Tourney Boosts Hamm's Foundation," *Washington Business Journal*, May 4, 2001.

"Hamm: Financial Support Strong for Women's Soccer," Interview, *Washington Business Journal*, Oct. 27, 2000.

"Hamm, U.S. Cruise to Win," Associated Press, August 12, 2004.

"It Went Down to the Wire: In a Dazzling World Cup Final, the Team that Captivated the Country Defeats China. Behind the Win – and How They're Taking Women's Sports to the Next Level," *Newsweek,* July 19, 1999.

"Mia Hamm," *Contemporary Heroes and Heroines.* Book IV, Gale Group, 2000.

"Mia Hamm: Gold Medal, Soccer," *People*, August 19, 1996.

"Mia Hamm (soccer player) (The 50 Most Beautiful People in the World 1997)," *People,* May 12, 1997.

"Mia Hamm: Soccer Superstar," http://transcripts.cnn.com, aired August 18, 2001.

"Mia Hamm to Carry U.S. Flag at Closing Ceremony," Associated Press, August 28, 2004.

"Mia Hamm: U.S. Soccer's Top Female Athlete Led the National Team in Goals and Assists," *Sports Illustrated for Kids,* January 1996.

"Profile: Mia Hamm," fifworldcup.com, 2003.

"Q&A with Bob Levey with Guests Mia Hamm and Abby Wambach," http://www.washingtonpost.com, August 5, 2003.

"Queries and Anecdotes: Mia Hamm," http://www.ussoccer.com, June 20, 2003.

"U.S. Outlasts Germany, Will Play Brazil for Gold," Associated Press, August 24, 2004.

Baker, John F. "Kate Morgan at HarperCollins Children's Books signed the world's top female soccer player, Mia Hamm, for an inspirational picture book called *Winners Never Quit,* to be illustrated by Carol Jackson," Publishers Weekly, February 2, 2004.

Carter, Gayle Jo. "The New Face of a Role Model," *USA Weekend Magazine,* June 20, 1999.

DeSimone, Bonnie. "All the World's a Stage for the Reluctant Star," *Chicago Tribune,* June 18, 1999.

Dure, Beau. "No Joy or Surprise in WUSA's Demise," *USA Today*, September 16. 2003.

Edelstein, Loren G. "A Hamm on Stage," *Meetings & Conventions*, August 2001.

Fee, Gayle, and Raposa, Laura. "Nomar, Mia Sign Life Contract," *Boston Herald*, November, 23, 2003.

Fowler, Scott. "Soccer Icon Mia Hamm Wants One More Gold for the Road," Knight-Ridder/Tribune News Service, July 26, 2004.

Gildea, William. "U.S. Effort Nets Second World Cup Title," *Washington Post*, July 11, 1999.

Haydon, John. "Mia Hamm Relishes Her Role as Big Cheese in Women's Game," *The Washington Times*, June 7, 1997.

——. "Mia's Difficult Year Ends on High Note," *The Washington Times*, December 22, 2001.

Hersh, Philip. "Era Ends: Germany Stuns U.S. in World Cup Semifinal," Knight-Ridder/Tribune News Service, October 5, 2003.

Horrigan, Jeff. "Garciaparra Angered Over WUSA Demise," *Boston Herald*, September 16, 2003.

Horovitz, Bruce. "Hamm's Popularity No Secret," *USA Today*, September 12, 2000.

Kaufman, Michelle. "U.S. Women's Soccer Team Preparing to Say Goodbye," Knight-Ridder/Tribune News Service, August 1, 2004.

Killian, Ann. "Mia Hamm Is Providing a Connection," Knight-Ridder/Tribune News Service, May 8, 1997.

Larson, Jennifer. "Having a Ball," _Seventeen_, June 1994.

Lewis, Michael. "Mia Hamm's Career Far From Over," http://www.scholastic.com, September 18, 2003.

Longman, Jere. "Show Time for Reluctant Soccer Superstar," _New York Times_, June 11, 1999.

———. "Hamm Is Well Known and Worn Out," _New York Times_, July 9, 1999.

———. "Hamm Is Comfortable in her Cleats Again," _New York Times_, June 15, 2003.

Mazzola, Gregg. "Goals (Interview with the World's Greatest Soccer Player, Mia Hamm)," _Coach and Athletic Director_, December 1998.

MacPherson, Brian. "Dorrance, Keller Resolve Sexual Harassment Lawsuit," _The Daily Tar Heel_, March 23, 2004.

MacQuarrie, Brian. "Hamm's Mate Trade in Sox Camps," Boston Globe, August 6, 2004.

Moore, David Leon. "Washington Claims WUSA Title," _USA Today_, August 24, 2003.

Plummer, William. "Goal Oriented: Mia Hamm Is College Soccer's Ms. Bigfoot," _People_, November 1, 1993.

Ponti, James. "Fast Forward: Mia Hamm of the U.S. Women's Soccer Team Runs Circles Around Opponents," _Sports Illustrated for Kids_, July 1995.

Posnanski, Joe. "In the End, Mia Was the One Who Was Golden," Knight-Ridder/Tribune News Service, August 28, 2004.

——. "Silver Medallists Are Champions," Knight Ridder/Tribune News Service, September 28, 2000.

Rooney, Marlene. "Good Sports: Meet One of the Helping Heroes of Sports," *Sports Illustrated for Kids*, December 1, 1999.

Shipley, Amy. "Loyalty, Sisterly Bond Help Spur Success," *Washington Post*, July 4, 1999.

Smith, Gary. "The Secret Life of Mia Hamm," *Sports Illustrated*, September 22, 2003.

Spence, Mike. "Mia Hamm Emerging as Best Female Soccer Player in the Year," Knight-Ridder/Tribune News Service, May 16, 1996.

Starr, Mark. "Keeping Her Own Score: The World Cup Will Show Everyone How Good Mia Hamm Is. Why Can't She See It?" *Newsweek*, June 21, 1999.

Voepel, Mechelle. "Hamm Has Been Better Than Ever So Far in the World Cup," Knight Ridder/Tribune News Service, September 30, 2003.

Wahl, Grant. "O Solo Mia: A New Take-Charge Mia Ham Led the U.S. into the Cup Quarterfinals," *Sports Illustrated*, October 6, 2003.

——. "Mia's Excellent Adventure," *Sports Illustrated for Women*, March 1, 2001.

White, Joseph. "Mia Hamm Ready to Go Out on Top at Worlds," Associated Press, September 17, 2003.

Whiteside, Kelly. "Norway out of Olympics after Loss to United States," *USA Today*, October 3, 2003.

Wright, Ken. "Different Goals for Mia Hamm after World Cup," *The Washington Times*, August 21, 2003.

Zindler, Ethan. "Kickin' It," Salon.com, June 23, 1999.

INDEX

Page numbers in *italics* indicate illustrations.

ABOUT THE AUTHOR

Joan Axelrod-Contrada is a freelance writer and author. She has written books for children about women leaders, the Lizzie Borden trial, and colonial America. She is also the author of *Career Opportunities in Politics, Government, and Activism* (Facts On File, 2003). As a freelance writer, she frequently contributes articles about career trends to the *Boston Globe.* She lives in western Massachusetts with her husband and two children.